Don't Make Me Come Up There!

Don't Make Me Come Up There!

KRISTEN WELCH

Quiet Moments
for Busy Moms

Abingdon Press
NASHVILLE

Don't Make Me Come Up There!
Quiet Moments for Busy Moms

This book is printed on acid-free paper.

Library of Congress Cataloging-in-Publication Data

Welch, Kristen.
    Don't make me come up there! : quiet moments for busy moms / Kristen Welch.
      p. cm.
    ISBN 978-1-4267-1222-7 (trade pbk. : alk. paper)
    1. Mothers—Prayers and devotions. 2. Christian women—Prayers and devotions. I. Title.
    BV4847.W44 2011
    242'.6431—dc22

                                          2010047835

11 12 13 14 15 16 17 18 19 20—10 9 8 7 6 5 4 3 2

MANUFACTURED IN THE UNITED STATES OF AMERICA

To my children:
MadiClaire, Jon-Avery, Emerson,
and Maureen, our "daughter" in Africa
Thank you for the constant inspiration and entertainment.
You are my delight.

To my husband:
You believed in me when I didn't believe in myself.
You are my heart.

To my Lord:
This is for your glory.

And special thanks to my mom,
who originally taught me the words,
"Don't Make Me Come Up There!"

And what does the LORD require of you?
To act justly and to love mercy
and to walk humbly with your God.
—Micah 6:8

Contents

Introduction

It had been quiet for too long. I stood with my hand on the banister and looked up the stairs at the closed bedroom doors. Nothing moved, and I couldn't hear a peep.

I couldn't help thinking of the last time my children had scattered up the stairs and disappeared into a quiet abyss. Initially, I thought they were just delighting in each other's company, holding hands, and making paper daisies. But that thought lasted for 1.2 seconds before I snapped out of my delusion only to discover my oldest giving her brother a "haircut" and my youngest smearing soap all over the bathroom.

My first two children were banished from scissors for all eternity, but it took me a while to clean up my toddler because she was locked in the bathroom. She had locked the door when she went in to use the bathroom. She was going to wash her hands with the soap and ended up scrubbing her body, the bathroom mirror, the walls, the door, and finally, the doorknob, making it too slippery to open.

So, I don't take quiet lightly. I called their names and waited for an answer. I screamed their names and still heard nothing. And that's when I said it: "Don't make me come up there!"

But they did. I'd waited long enough, so I climbed over the toys that trickled down the stairs and quietly tiptoed to the first two doors, only to discover the rooms empty. I mentally prepared myself for the possibility of bald children (or worse) as I turned the knob of the third door. My verbal arsenal was ready to unload on my sneaky children. I was certain they were up to no good.

I gasped . . . to discover all three of my kids piled up in the bed, tucked under covers, with my oldest reading quietly to her siblings. Her boom box was playing music in the background, and I couldn't help wondering: *what happened to MY kids?*

All sets of eyes looked up from their paper adventure, and my son said, "Hi, Mom. Did you need something?"

"No, just checking on you guys. Keep reading," I said as I closed the door quickly so I wouldn't disturb the rare moment of perfection. I closed my eyes, sealing in the memory. Because, let's face it, this could have gone either way.

If you've ever wondered if it was safe to go into your child's room, locked yourself in the bathroom for a personal time-out, or felt ridiculously proud and horrified (all in the same hour) at your children's behavior, this book is for you.

I'm a mom. I'm not an expert on parenting (but I can nurse a baby while loading the dishwasher and clip tiny fingernails while reading a bedtime story!). I know how stressful being a mom can be: balancing duties, caring for needs, and loving them so much it hurts.

Becoming a mother is one of the most precious gifts God has given me. And after I traveled to Africa, he added the gift of perspective. I talk a lot about both in the following pages. I've found that all the little ups and downs in motherhood are easier to handle when I have the right perspective.

You won't find all your parenting questions answered in this book, but you will find a mom who knows what it's like to long for a quiet moment alone with her thoughts and her heavenly Father. I wrote this for book for you, and I wrote it *for me*.

1

If the Mom Genes Fit

When I first started birthing babes, I was shocked at how hard it was to juggle everything. I'm not just talking about playdates, housework, and school projects.

I mean literally, juggling a diaper bag, a 100-pound baby carrier—not including a baby whose thighs resemble those of a small Sumo wrestler—and a purse, all while trying to keep a two-year-old from scraping gum off the sidewalk.

I've always thought that with the title *Mother* we should grow an extra appendage or two. Because, seriously, an extra arm would come in handy when I'm stirring dinner, loading the dishwasher, calling out multiplication facts, stepping over the mock kitchen my toddler has created underfoot, and paying bills online—*simultaneously*.

In one day, I accomplish more than some small companies. Heck, I am a small company. I've spent a combined total of nearly forty hours in labor delivering more than twenty pounds of human.

When I became a mother, I put on the mom jeans and developed mom genes. I can hear my baby blink in the middle of the night, read my tween's mind when she's giving me a dirty look, and unlatch a nursing bra without my hands.

And I'll be honest, when someone has the nerve to ask me in a questioning tone, "What do you *do* all day?" I've decided this will be my forever answer: "I'm a mom. What's your superpower?"

God created mothers to nurture, protect, and love their children unconditionally. He understands that children are their mother's heart because he designed us that way. When our tanks are empty and exhaustion is our middle name, God is the one who says, "Come to me. I will give you rest."

Lean on him. It's in our nature to do it all, but when we can't go on, he is there to sustain us. He is there in the middle of the night when our kids are sick. He is there when we don't know how to discipline. He is there when one goes astray.

As much as we love our children, he loves them more. Trust him.

Proverbs 3:5

Trust in the LORD with all your heart
   and lean not on your own understanding.

Prayer

Lord, sometimes I feel invincible and sometimes I feel exhausted from trying to do it all myself. Help me trust you with my kids and with my own life. Thank you for making me a mother. Give me strength to accomplish all that you've set before me and give me joy in my journey. Amen.

2

They Will Let Anyone Be a Mom These Days

I was leisurely scrolling through the latest posts of the blogs I read every day. I was unbathed and pajama-clad. (Actually, I had lost my pajama bottoms somewhere along the way of rushing my older kids out the door, so I was half naked.) My priorities were in order: I was reading other people's business before I took care of my own.

My one-year-old sat in my lap while I worked on my laptop at the kitchen counter. My baby dug through the kitchen drawer as I intently read. She started squirming, so I sat her on the floor with a piece of plastic in her hand. At least that's what I thought it was, until she started screaming.

I whipped around and IN SLOW MOTION BECAUSE I'M A SLOW THINKER realized that the said plastic was SUPER GLUE, which was now dripping and full of teeth marks. I scooped her up and ran to the kitchen sink.

These words began flashing in my head: YOU ARE NOT MATURE ENOUGH TO BE A MOTHER. FIND AN ADULT IMMEDIATELY.

My daughter's hands were covered in Super Glue and her lips were glued closed.

Let me just pause and let that sink in: Baby. Lips. Glued together *for eternity*. Jesus, help me.

I'm crying. She's crying. I'm splashing water on both of us, praying for help, and begging for forgiveness. It did dawn on me in a surreal way how perfectly still my child became. She knew it was bad. And I think she was hoping for another adult to arrive.

The warm water and a little pressure helped part her crusty lips. THANK GOD. She didn't ingest the glue, and that seemed to be very good news.

I nearly passed out when I heard the key in the front door.

A host of heavenly angels ushered my dear hubby into the kitchen in search of something he'd forgotten. He saw the Super Glue, our crusty hands, and his baby's lips and took over.

I googled "baby lips and super glue," which I'm sure helped child protective services home in on my whereabouts. *And* I'm sure this was an Internet first.

According to reliable resources, acetone is the enemy to Super Glue. It's the kryptonite to the super mega adhesive. We dipped cotton into nail polish remover and scrubbed. Our one-year-old perfected her dirty look, and my husband didn't even ask how it happened.

"I've got to get to work," my husband said as he grabbed his jacket.

"What? You can't leave me. I cannot be trusted. It's not even 8:30 a.m. and I nearly wounded your baby," I said as I grabbed his pant leg and held on for dear life. He smiled at me. And left.

Have you ever felt unqualified to be a mom? I made a mistake that could have caused severe injury to my child and I couldn't get past the guilt. I was horrified at my negligence and berated myself until I finally had a good cry in the tub. I reminded myself that I wasn't a bad mom, just human. But God reminded me that I wasn't alone. He equips us to handle the tough mom stuff, the things in the future we can't even imagine. He won't give us more than we can handle.

Don't be too hard on yourself. It isn't an accident that you're a mom. God will enable you!

1 Samuel 25:28

Please forgive your servant's offense, for the LORD will certainly make a lasting dynasty for my master, because he fights the LORD's battles. Let no wrongdoing be found in you as long as you live.

Prayer

God, thank you for your protection. Please watch over those I love. Guard them with your angels. Keep my spouse and my children safe from harm. Amen.

3

The Magic Eraser

Confession: sometimes I ignore my children. The other day, I was busy at my computer. My kids were home from school and done with their homework. Usually, I'm rushing around getting snacks, going through backpack papers, and trying to decide what to make for dinner with one potato, two cans of corn, and a link of sausage. Instead, I was in cyberspace.

My kids asked if they could use my giant box of Sharpie markers for coloring. Now, every mother knows you don't let your young children color with permanent markers. But shopping on the Internet for squeaky shoes for your toddler who isn't toddling can distort this. I said yes. *So it seems.*

About twenty minutes later, I looked up to see my children at the dining room table coloring away.

"What do you think you are doing?" I demanded, vaguely remembering I had approved their activity.

When I looked closer, I freaked out. Underneath the notebook paper was an entire scene of flowers, bugs, and robots in permanent marker on my beautiful table.

I am not proud of what happened next: I yelled. I screamed. *I shook my fists in the air!*

My daughter rolled her eyes at me and said, "You said it was OK," and stormed off to her room. My son's lips trembled, and he burst into tears. He grabbed my legs and begged forgiveness. He then slowly walked to his room with his head bent in sorrow.

I let my kids walk away.

Grabbing a rag and furniture polish, I scrubbed and didn't remove the ink. Digging through my stash of cleaners, I found a "Magic Eraser." It was unopened, and I needed some magic. I wet it and wiped the table. *Every mark disappeared.*

"Kids, kids come here. Look, it's magic," I exclaimed.

No one came.

That's when it dawned on me that I was a horrible mother. I brought each of my children downstairs. I showed them the magic. My daughter, with arms crossed, said, "That's cool, I guess." My son's shoulders still shook.

"It's OK," I said.

He burst into tears. "I'm sorry," he cried.

I got down on my knees and pulled my kids to me. This is what I said:

"I was wrong. I made a mistake. I shouldn't have let you use those markers, or I should have put a tablecloth down first. I'm sorry for yelling and blaming you. It was not your fault. Can you forgive me?"

My daughter shrugged and my son sniffled.

"I sinned," I confessed.

They both looked up at me. Surprise registered on their faces.

"I forgive you," my daughter said. "Me, too," my son whimpered as he wiped his runny nose.

They left me standing in the kitchen. I picked up the eraser to put it away. I still felt bad and angry with myself. I looked at the eraser and wished I could swipe it across my heart to remove the awful residue.

And then I remembered, I can.

We make mistakes. We feel bad, even sorry. We ask forgiveness. The sin is wiped away. Just like that. The Magic Eraser: I got to use two of them in one day. And I am thankful for both.

Psalm 51:7

Cleanse me with hyssop, and I will be clean;
  wash me, and I will be whiter than snow.

Prayer

Father, I am so human. I make so many mistakes. Please forgive me. Help me forgive myself when I mess up. I need your help. I can't do this on my own. Be strong when I am weak. Amen.

4

The Bad Guys

We went and saw Bibleman in a live show the other night at our church. Bibleman is a superhero who uses Scripture to defeat the bad guys. Nearly every kid in the auditorium was dressed in a purple and yellow cape, with a mask.

Of course, in *our* family, we *never* lower ourselves to the lure of commercialization.

But she looked so cute in her purple cape.

Our kids have been defeating bad guys with their lightsabers and (their interpretation of) the word of God all week. Our toddler has a mask and some anonymity.

After some deep thoughts, she asked her sister if Bibleman was bad.

"No," our older daughter said. "Jesus lives in his heart, just like he lives in your heart."

Our two-year-old thought about that for a minute and shook her head *no*.

"Who lives in your heart then?" our nine-year-old asked her baby sister.

"The bad guys," our toddler said.

There are days I would completely agree. I'm just sayin'.

Our older kids have been trying to convince her to get saved all week.

She wants no part of it. Because she and the bad guys *are living it up*.

I've learned more about God and his grace from my kids than I learned in Bible college! They just say it like they see it. I love their honesty, and frankly, they are hilarious. I want to raise them to be Christians, but it's more than making them conform to what we think Christians should do and say. It starts with a transformation *to* Christianity rather than conformity. Guess who their model is? Yep.

There have been times that I freaked out when my kids acted especially unholy in front of other people. But it's OK to let them be themselves. We need to remember that even Christian kids sin. It's really the heart and the transformation that matter.

Romans 12:2

Do not conform any longer to the pattern of this world, but be transformed by the renewing of your mind.

Prayer

Father, I want to raise my kids to know you. I want them to have their own relationship with you. But sometimes I'm so caught up in making them act like Christians that I forget even Christian kids mess up. Give me wisdom in raising them and help me be the same at home and at church. Amen.

5

Sometimes I Want to Quit

I like to think about good things.

I like to remind people they aren't alone.

I like to remind myself.

I try not to rant and carry on about the things I feel negative about.

I don't intend to start now.

But sometimes I just want to quit.

I hate even writing those words because I'm not a quitter.

I don't intend to start now.

But sometimes the *want* is there.

We've made an effort to teach our kids to be thankful. It seems, when we focus on this, a spirit of being unthankful and complain-with-every-breath sweeps through our house. It rears its ugly head more than I care to admit.

And when I plan special activities for my kids and they whine and gripe, I want to beat them.

I don't intend to start now.

My life is messy. It's not the clean, crisp (edited) life you always see. I yell (!) sometimes. I cry and dream of a full-time nanny. At times I feel guilty and sad and completely unequipped.

And even though it may sound pathetic, I *want* to be what others think I am. I set the bar high, occasionally I scale it, but usually I end up missing it entirely.

Being a mom is hard.

I don't intend to *stop* now.

I am not a quitter. I'm going to complete what I've started. I know I'm going to have bad days. I'm not perfect and neither is my family, but I'm not going to give up on them or myself.

So, the next time you're ready to throw in the towel and turn in your dishpan hands, remember that motherhood isn't defined by a single act or one bad day. It's cumulative: it's a thousand hugs, a thousand apologies, a thousand times you are there for your kids. You probably won't ever get credit for all you give, but he is keeping count and giving you the grace you need to continue.

1 Corinthians 9:24

Do you not know that in a race all the runners run, but only one gets the prize? Run in such a way as to get the prize.

Prayer

Heavenly father, help me run with perseverance. When I get tired, encourage me. When I want to quit, carry me to the finish line. Thank you for being so faithful to me. Amen.

6

Just Send Me Your Therapy Bills

I think I've failed my children.

You be the judge: at breakfast this past weekend, something had obviously been bothering my son because between bites of scrambled eggs he said, "Mom, why didn't you tell me I was a mammal? I didn't find out until I was in *kindergarten*."

And considering he is now halfway through the first grade, I'd say he's been holding this in for a while.

My third-grade daughter offered her mammal opinion:

"Well. It doesn't even matter because *you* are not a mammal. You don't feed your young milk from your body, do you?" she asked. "Plus, the dolphin is the smartest mammal."

Well there you go.

Strangely, that got me off the hook. And no, I didn't even correct her. It's certainly NOT because I don't know my mammal facts. I do. *I think*.

Later that day, my kids were playing with action figures and I heard some smashing and crashing.

And then I heard this: "Oh, no, he fell. He is really hurt. He is really suffering!"

"You know what this means, don't you?"

"Yeah, we'll have to put the guy out of his misery since he's hurt so bad." And then I heard all sorts of frightening sounds.

Did my kids just choose *euthanasia* for a parachuting action figure? I'll just add that talk to my to-do list. But just in case there are permanent effects from this recent behavior, I'll have them send their therapy bills to me.

Sometimes I worry about my lack of parenting skills. Since I'm learning as I go, I pray that God will fill in all the pieces I miss and protect my children from my mistakes.

They belong to him anyway. I forget that. God created my children. He's giving me the honor of raising them, but he is ordering their steps. He took care in making them:

Psalm 139:14

I praise you because I am fearfully and wonderfully made;
> your works are wonderful,
> I know that full well.

He will order their steps:

Proverbs 20:24

A man's steps are directed by the LORD.
> How then can anyone understand his own way?

Prayer

God, please protect my children. Protect them from my mistakes and from their own. Keep them healthy and safe. Guard their hearts in Christ Jesus. Give me wisdom as their mother. Amen.

7

Is That Bad?

A friend and I stopped by Chick-fil-A the other day. I leaned into the speaker and ordered a large sweet tea.

"OK, Kristen. That's $1.67," the speaker answered.

As I pulled around, I could feel my friend staring at me.

"What?" I asked.

"That lady, in the speaker, *she knew your name!*" she said in disbelief.

"Oh, that. Yeah, I come here. A lot. It's funny, she recognizes my voice now and . . ." my words trailed off because she was really staring now. Intensely.

"What? Oh, *is that bad*?" I asked guiltily.

It never dawned on me that it wasn't normal for fast-food restaurants to recognize you *before* they saw you.

Besides knowing my name and debit card number, the Chick-fil-A lady frequently comments on how easy it is to make sweet tea at *home* and how *fattening* it is.

I still go back, even though I know it's not the healthiest habit. I do it because it's important to me. It's a simple moment in my day or week that's about me. I have to remind myself that it isn't bad to think about myself in this busy mothering season I'm in.

What do you do for yourself? Do you take a moment for you? In order to refill the demanding souls around us, we need to focus on ourselves every once in a while. Our kids aren't afraid to ask for what they need, usually with persistence. Moms need to acknowledge the needs in their own lives: a moment alone, time away, a girls' night out, or a sweet tea (that you don't have to share!).

Remember that thinking about you every now and then isn't bad. It's necessary.

I challenge you to do something for yourself this week. Take time to mark it on the calendar, plan it in the budget. Make yourself a priority and do so without guilt. Guilt steals joy, and you'll feel better about yourself and your mothering when you focus on YOU.

Romans 8:1-2

Therefore, there is now no condemnation for those who are in Christ Jesus, because through Christ Jesus the law of the Spirit of life set me free from the law of sin and death.

Prayer

Sometimes I'm plagued with guilt, Lord. I know this isn't from you. Thank you for setting me free from condemnation—from others and from myself. Remind me to take time for myself because I need it. I love you. Amen.

8

Turns Out We Are Dirty People

My teeth have low self-esteem. I have a long history of dental problems that have resulted in a phobia of sorts. But I want my kids to have healthy teeth and positive feelings about their dental hygiene experience, so I push past my fears and take them to the dentist twice a year like I'm supposed to, although I find this nearly as bad as taking myself to the dentist because you know whom they blame when your children have cavities. *Oh, goody, more mom guilt. Thank you very much.*

I like to prepare myself for ten cavities each. I like to go there mentally, just in case. I like dealing with worst-case scenarios head-on.

It was much worse than I had feared. I mean so bad I might need counseling or a beer, which is saying a lot, since I'm the wife of a former pastor and get tipsy from NyQuil.

Oh, no, my kids didn't have ten cavities; they had . . . wait for it . . .

None! Not one cavity; totally clear, beautifully clean teeth.

But apparently that's *nothing* because by the look on the hygienist's face, I knew there was something else. She quietly leaned in and said for adult ears only, "Your daughter has *lice*."

Let's just let that nugget sink in. Um, no thank you, my kids don't get lice. *LICE*: as in bugs dwelling in your scalp. Only to be *discovered by a dental hygienist.*

DON'T MAKE ME COME UP THERE!

Turns out my deep conviction that only dirty people get lice is not true. Or is it? Thank God for over-the-counter hair pesticide.

On the bright side, I've learned there's *much more* to fear than cavities during a simple visit to the dentist.

That day goes down in history as one of the worst! We all have them, don't we? It was embarrassing for me, humiliating for my daughter, expensive, and long. I remember falling in bed, exhausted! God used this day to humble me. He reminded me that being clean on the outside doesn't always mean being clean on the inside. My pride left a dirty stain on my heart. But the great thing about serving an amazing God is a fresh start every day, a clean slate. He makes all things new, forgives our mistakes, encourages us through the hard moments, and restores hope.

Lamentations 3:22-24

Because of the LORD's great love we are not consumed,
    for his compassions never fail.
  They are new every morning;
    great is your faithfulness.
  I say to myself, "The LORD is my portion;
    therefore I will wait for him."

Prayer

Father, some days are just hard. I grow so tired and get frustrated. But your love renews me. Your mercy offers me a new day, a fresh start. Thank you for the gift of a clean start. Amen.

9

I'm Sorry

My little boy is sensitive. He is sandwiched between two sisters. His heart is big, generous, and he's an encourager by nature.

But I've noticed he says two things all the time.

First (and totally not his fault), he says "Omygosh" every time he's excited, shocked, surprised, happy, mad.

In other words, he says it *a lot*. So does his momma. And I'm working on that. Really, I am. Especially since my toddler picked it up the other day. It sounds horrible coming from her baby lips.

But the other phrase he uses often is "I'm sorry."

In his sweet way, whenever he's corrected or asked something, he tucks his head, looks down, and says "I'm sorry" first.

I decided I really needed to help him understand that "I am sorry" is an apology. It's not what you say when you think you might be in trouble or when you're slow to make your bed or when you ask if you can stay up a few minutes to read.

I talked with him and explained that he didn't have to be sorry for everything. I encouraged him to use those words only when he needed to apologize.

A few nights later, we worked in the yard after dinner. We came in hot and tired. I was ready for a bath after my kids had theirs. I was also ready for them to get to bed.

My son entered the kitchen and said, "Can I have a snack?"

"I guess," I exhaled.

"I'm sorry," he said.

I stopped him. "Why? Why are you sorry for asking for a snack? You've worked hard and you're hungry."

"I said I'm sorry because of the look on your face. You looked very sad when I asked you," he confessed.

And that's when it dawned on me. My little boy apologizes *for me*, not *to me*. My actions, the look on my face, my tone, make him feel as though he has wronged me in some way.

I cringed at my own discovery. Countless memories, tones, and apologies flooded my head.

I hugged his gangly body to mine and told him *I* was sorry. "I'm sorry for making you feel like you were doing something wrong. I'm tired, honey, and I'm ready to go to bed. It's not you. It's me."

It's in those little moments that I feel God's finger pinpointing a place in my heart, an ugly spot that I need to work on.

My exasperation and moods affect my kids. My tone and impatient foot tapping make them feel pressured and uncomfortable.

It was me all along.

And I'm sorry.

2 Thessalonians 2:16-17

May our Lord Jesus Christ himself and God our Father, who has loved us and given us everlasting comfort and hope which we don't deserve, comfort your hearts with all comfort, and help you in every good thing you say and do. *(The Living Bible)*

Prayer

Jesus, you know me. There are no secrets with you. I can't hide who I am, and sometimes, I'm just a sinful mess. I'm sorry for my sinful ways, for my bad moods and sharp tongue. Help me show grace and mercy to others and become more like you. Amen.

10

A Crime Investigation

I love garage sales. As a teen, I used to shop in secondhand stores for my clothes because I wanted to. I didn't even consider this a problem.

Right now, I'm on home-decor probation, so I usually shop for my kids instead.

As I combed the sale, I looked for something I could take home that would be fun. I found it: a complete (new in the box) CSI Crime Investigation Kit, complete with finger printing. Retail value $99.00. I got it for eight bucks.

My kids were thrilled! They were occupied for hours, you know, creating crimes and then solving them. It was a hoot. I enjoyed it until they brought this special light that detects liquid or bodily fluids, as my daughter stated.

I know. Just typing that made me shiver.

They donned their plastic gloves and protective eye gear and went to work: ON MY HOUSE. This is what I heard over and over: "Oooooh! Gross. Look at that."

"Oh, what till you see this! That is disgusting."

It went on and on. And then it dawned on me: *They are not pretending.*

Surely that toy light is not detecting something in my house? Then I heard, "She really needs to clean this house."

I jumped up and did some of my own investigating.

I found my two punks in their bathroom hovering over "evidence."

"All right, all right, let me see," I said and grabbed the light.

GAAASSSP! I shone the light onto the wall and exposed pee in a sprinkled pattern. I held it over the commode and, yep, you guessed it, little illuminated dots.

"See, we told you," they said in unison.

"You really oughta do something about this," my daughter demanded.

I handed her the light and returned a few minutes later with an array of cleaning supplies.

"This is a true investigation. Clues are pointing to you." I handed them a rag and said, "Since you've got your rubber gloves on, it's time to clean up this crime scene."

I wasn't so much the "best mom ever" anymore from the look on my kids' faces, but their bathroom glistened, until someone had to potty again.

This is not unlike my heart at times. It looks clean on the outside, but I'm a mess on the inside. Grumbling, complaining, and gossiping have left my heart stained with sin. I'm able to keep it covered and maybe unknown, until it's exposed to the Light.

Jesus exposes the dark places. But he doesn't do it to make me feel bad or unclean; he does it because he is the perfect cleanser. He washes it away, so the inside washes the outside.

1 John 1:6-8

If we claim to have fellowship with him yet walk in the darkness, we lie and do not live by the truth. But if we walk in the light, as he is in the light, we have fellowship with one another, and the blood of Jesus, his Son, purifies us from all sin. If we claim to be without sin, we deceive ourselves and the truth is not in us.

Prayer

Lord, please help me search my heart. I know there are some places that need to be cleaned. Would you shine your light on the dark spots of pride and cleanse me? Thank you, Jesus, for your powerful blood. Amen.

11

I Will Not Leave You

Son, I'm going to grab a quick bath, OK?"

"Uh-huh," he mumbled from the middle of my bed, surrounded by big pillows and covered in thick blankets.

He was taking a sick day from school, and the rest of the family was in the school drop-off line. I decided to grab the few minutes of quiet because I knew they would be fleeting.

I shut the door with my son on the other side, ran a hot bath, and slipped into the tub. The warm water eased my harried mind. In the quiet, I closed my eyes. A few minutes passed.

And that's when I heard an urgent, guttural cry, a scream for help.

I jumped from the water, grabbed my towel, and threw open the door. I found my feverish son standing in the middle of my room, shaking and crying in fear.

"What? What happened? Are you OK?" I glanced around the room with a pounding heart.

Through sobs and snotty tears: "I couldn't find you. I couldn't find you. I couldn't find you," he repeated over and over.

"Son, I was in the bath! Why did you think I left?" I said with a trembling voice.

"I don't know. I just forgot. Sometimes I'm afraid I will be left alone and not have you and Daddy," he sobbed uncontrollably.

I grabbed him by the arms and peered into his eyes and said with all the love and firmness I possessed, "I will not leave. I WILL NOT leave you. I WILL NOT LEAVE YOU."

And then I hugged him, and we both cried.

Even after I'd comforted him, the words banged around in my heart: *I will not leave you.* Once I'd settled my son back in bed, my hubby returned home with our toddler to grab a few items and head to work. I told him what happened.

Understandably, he thought it was ridiculous that my son knew I was taking a bath only to forget and get hysterical for no reason. He blamed it on his not feeling well. I agreed.

But I couldn't shake those words from my head. So, I sat down and listened to my heart.

This is what I heard: "I will not leave you, Kristen. I will not leave you. Even though you know I am here, you doubt me. Some days you feel alone, isolated, and afraid. I will not leave you. I WILL NOT leave you. I WILL NOT LEAVE YOU."

It was as if God grabbed me by the arms, peered into my eyes, and said it with all the love and firmness he possessed.

And I believed him.

Isaiah 12:2

Surely God is my salvation;

I will trust and not be afraid.

The LORD, the LORD, is my strength and my song;

he has become my salvation.

Prayer

Thank you, Jesus, for being my strength and my salvation. You have saved me from so much. You continue to rescue me from my own doubts and fears. Help me lean on you in all things. Amen.

1 2

When I Fail

Last week was bad. Not the kind of bad you can blame on a broken dishwasher or a naughty child or someone else.

It was a week filled with me *failing*.

I wasn't a great mom or a good wife. I raised my voice too much and didn't listen enough. I was short-tempered and impatient and just generally unhappy.

Sure, I can come up with excuses that might justify some of my behavior. But I had a choice how to handle my frustrating week. And I *failed*. It hurts to admit that I had a test and I got a big fat zero on it.

We live in a world that doesn't like failure. It's ugly and messy. Our world wants perfection, perfectly manicured people who never mess up. Just turn on the television or go to the movies or ask a friend if he or she has messed up lately.

When you do fail, there are always a handful of people to point it out, especially in the church. Just think about the pastors and TV evangelists who've suffered a public fall. It fills the news. Failure makes us uncomfortable. Failure makes us want to cover it up, excuse it. Failure makes us want to run away.

But we were created to fail. We were born imperfect and into sin.

Through failure, I am drawn to the one who *runs to me*. He does not turn away from my shortcomings. He is not afraid of my humanity.

My pastor explained this so clearly one Sunday morning: When I cut my hand chopping veggies in the kitchen, the blood in my body rushes out of the wound. That's what it was created to do. Our blood was designed to wash out the impurities and clot to protect us.

When I fail as a parent or a wife or a person, his blood goes to my injured heart. It rushes to the place I hurt. Because that's what it was created to do.

He is there to wash away my regret and my sin when I fail.

Psalm 51:10

Create in me a pure heart, O God,
and renew a steadfast spirit within me.

Prayer

God, I'm so thankful that you specialize in messes. You are good at fixing broken things. I give myself to you, all the successes and all the failures. Please purify me and create a clean heart in me. Amen.

1 3

The Lost and the Found

I stood on the crowded concrete sidewalk looking for my oldest two in the throngs of children bursting through the school doors. Spotted, their eyes find mine and ask the same question that comes each day, "Can we stay and play?"

I nod my head; they drop backpacks at my feet, grab their baby sister's hand, and run to the swings. I find a spot to sit and visit with other mothers.

It doesn't take long for my toddler to find a mud puddle from the rains that soaked the ground the day before. I collect her shoes and tug her resistant hand. It's time for homework and time to stir dinner in the Crock-Pot.

My oldest helps with the youngest, and I search the playing field for my son. I don't see him. I ask his sisters. They look, too, calling and looking.

Searching. Looking. Pacing. He is not there. I try to slow the heart that beats faster with that very thought.

I ask around and pick up my pace, trying to remember if the shirt he wore today is yellow or orange. The crowd has thinned, but my voice is thick.

I call his name. I search and grab my phone. Others are hunting him, too. And then I look into the future of a life without my son. I pray that thought away.

Suddenly, he stumbles toward me from a forbidden wooded area that surrounds the elementary school. I can tell by his trembling lip and his older sister's stern face, he knew my heart was in my throat.

"I'm sorry, Mom," he cried. This is my sensitive one. With just a look, he crumbles. I hugged him close, taking in the scent of this one-day man. Tears formed and I blinked them away.

He continued to apologize until we got home. I accepted it over and over. "What happened? You know that you aren't supposed to go into the woods. I thought you were lost."

Wiping his nose on his sleeve, he said, "I didn't know I was lost. Some friends asked me to come with them to help collect pine needles. I knew I shouldn't. I gave in to temptation," he said as he hugged me tight, willing my forgiveness. I hid my smile and my tears in his hair.

"You are forgiven. But you disobeyed." I doled out a consequence (a small one since he had already punished himself so severely).

Later as I recounted the event, I saw it differently. I was the lost. Searching for something unimportant in a place I shouldn't be. Trying to do things on my own, pleasing the people around me, giving in to temptation.

But God was searching for me. He was calling my name. Even now, when I stumble off the path, neglect the word, seek fortune, and altogether fail, he rallies a search party, shines his light into the darkness of my selfishness, and draws me near.

He leaves the ninety-nine for the one. Me.

Luke 15:4

Suppose one of you has a hundred sheep and loses one of them. Does he not leave the ninety-nine in the open country and go after the lost sheep until he finds it?

Prayer

God, you love us so much that you sent Jesus to seek the lost. He seeks even the one, even me. Thank you, Jesus, for helping when I wander off-track. You are always there leading me, looking for me. Thank you, Jesus. Amen.

14

I Lied

My in-laws made the long drive down to Texas for a visit. They are farmers and aren't able to come very often, so it was a special treat, especially for my kids.

They came in late Thursday and were driving back home early Sunday morning. Since it was such a quick trip, I decided to keep my kids home from school on Friday so we could take a day trip. I wanted my kids to have as much time as possible with their grandparents.

We had a wonderful weekend (which included a community garage sale and *many* desserts)!

I didn't give much thought to my kids' absence until it was time to write a note to the school. And that's when I remembered that all grades given on days of unexcused absences (everything except sickness and doctor's visits are unexcused) result in a maximum of a 70 percent grade.

So, basically, if my kids missed a day of school, the most they could make for any grade taken that day (including my daughter's big English test) would be a 70 because of an unexcused absence.

Dumb rule.

So, I wrote on the note, "Please excuse my children from being absent; they were under the weather."

I completely justified it. I convinced myself that it was OK because they were my kids and it was a good reason.

I played the situation over in my head enough to feel OK about it, until my son got home from school on Monday.

"Mom? Today, I felt really weird. My teacher asked me why I missed school and wanted to know if I felt better. My stomach was in knots, and I didn't know what to say," he struggled to say.

And that's when it hit me. I lied. I didn't exaggerate or stretch the truth or bend the rules for a good cause. I lied.

I started explaining to my son about the rule and grades and—I stopped.

What exactly was I trying to say? That it's OK to lie if you don't like the rules? It's OK to work around guidelines we don't agree with or think dumb? Or worse, that a 70 percent on a test isn't good enough?

I grabbed him by the hand and said, "Son, I lied. I'm sorry. I didn't like the rule at school, so I tried to get around it. It's my fault you felt that way. Will you forgive me for putting you in that situation?" And then I added, "Next time, just tell the teacher your mom kept you home." He actually heaved a sigh of relief.

I beat myself up about getting caught in a lie by my own child! I've forgiven myself, God has forgiven me, and I'm thankful for the opportunity for growth.

Parenting is hard work, especially when you're the model. I'm not perfect, and even though my kids know that I'm not perfect, it's not easy confessing to them. But I took it a step further; I also notified the school of my mistake.

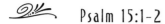 ## Psalm 15:1-2

LORD, who may dwell in your sanctuary?
  Who may live on your holy hill?
He whose walk is blameless
  and who does what is righteous,
who speaks the truth from his heart.

Prayer

Oh, heavenly father, my own righteousness is like filthy rags. I'm so full of my own ideas and thoughts that sometimes I don't make room for you. I want to be blameless. I want to walk straight in front of my kids without leading them astray, but I can only do this if I follow you. Amen.

15

This Is Where I Hide in the Garage

I'm not good at keeping in touch. It may be a character flaw. As a matter of fact, until I joined Facebook due to peer pressure, I hadn't stayed in touch with one high school friend. (Also, I still give in to peer pressure.)

So, I pretty much ignored the first three e-mails I got from my high school alumni group asking me to update my information for our twenty-year reunion in 2010.

But then I got The Yellow Card in the mail saying I would be deleted from the directory if I didn't respond. And even though I didn't care, I didn't really want to cease to exist.

So, I decided to call while I was preparing dinner and had all three kids in the kitchen. I like to use my brain like that.

As I was confirming my address and my college degree, my toddler began shrieking to get out of her high chair. I walked to the other room and tried to hear the woman's question.

The screaming ensued. I put the lady on hold and put my toddler on the floor. Full. Blown. Tantrum. So, I did what any sane mother would do: I shut the kids behind the baby gate (a.k.a. the safe part of the house) and went to the garage.

"What is your occupation? Do you work from home?" the lady asked.

Panic. Because this is where I had to pretend to be successful. "I'm a writer."

"Oh, really? Great, I'll put that under occupation. What do you write?"

Shoot.

"Various things," I said vaguely.

"There's a place for a URL," she pressed.

"I'm a blogger." I then proceeded to give her the name of my blog, but I couldn't concentrate because I could hear my kids through the garage door. The screaming was getting closer. *They could smell my fear.*

"We are THAT family dot com," I spelled out.

"That sounds interesting," she responded. *Oh, yes, that's one way to put it.*

And then after I agreed to a copy of the directory, the lady kicked it up a notch and started the sales pitch. In order to reserve my copy, I had to pay at that exact moment.

Knocking on the garage door began.

"I can't right now. Can I call you back and pay later?" I begged.

The lady offered me "three more choices: payment plans," yada, yada, yada.

Banging.

"Really. I can't right now." I was pleading, but I still had my successful voice on.

"If this is a money issue—" she began.

The doorknob was turning. The Children had found me.

"Listen, it's not necessarily a money issue except that if I buy one, it will be the cheapest choice you offer. But I'm in my garage right now. I'm hiding from my hysterical children. AND I DO NOT HAVE MY PURSE IN HERE AND THERE IS NO WAY I CAN GO GET IT RIGHT NOW. OK?"

Successful voice had been replaced with ALL-CAPS VOICE.

"Oh. Yes. I see. You really are THAT family. I hope you make a lot of money writing about your life."

Have you ever needed to escape? I can't tell you how many phone conversations I've had locked away in my closet or bathroom. These quiet, small places have been a momentary refuge from the chaos that is my life at times. They are temporary, though.

But there is a great refuge. He is always available. He is big enough to hide within. I can take my worries, my doubt, and my humiliation to him. There is no judgment or chastisement. He offers me unconditional love, acceptance, and peace.

Run to him.

Psalm 91:1-3

He who dwells in the shelter of the Most High
    will rest in the shadow of the Almighty.
I will say of the LORD, "He is my refuge and my fortress,
    my God, in whom I trust."
Surely he will save you from the fowler's snare
    and from the deadly pestilence.

(We all know there is occasional "deadly pestilence," don't we?)

Prayer

Jesus, my life can be chaotic, and there are times I seek refuge from the noise and I just need a break. Instead of turning to other things in my life, please help me remember that you are my refuge. You are my shelter. Amen.

16

What We're About

As we munched on lemon–poppy seed muffins the morning of the second day of school, we tuned in to our local Christian radio station.

Over breakfast, we listened to my first radio interview. The local radio station discovered that we were "paying our kids to read the Bible." It all started with a little challenge my husband gave to our kids: he offered them a big reward if they could read their entire children's Bible over the summer.

Our second-grade son completed it first. We believe God loves to reward his children. We just took our cue from him (and it really developed a great love for the Bible in our children).

My son and hubby beamed as the radio played; my toddler pointed to the radio and kept saying, "Momma in de radio." I flinched at the sound of my voice over the airwaves, and our nine-year-old daughter pouted, acting like she wasn't the least bit interested in the excitement.

Our strong, independent girl is an achiever. She completes tasks, is a hard worker, and is a leader. But she didn't feel as motivated as her brother to read her Bible. And that was OK with me (no pressure challenge), but it wasn't OK with her.

Being a parent is hard. With one side of my heart, I celebrated my son and his accomplishment. But the other part of my heart broke for my oldest, in the grip of jealousy.

I pulled her aside and looked into her tear-filled eyes. "I know this is hard. I know you wish it were you. And I'm sorry. But we are going to celebrate your brother. We are going to gather around him and we are going to be proud, just like we did with you when you made the Fun Run team. And when you finish reading your Bible—even if it's a year from now—we will celebrate you! We're a family."

And then I hugged her and cried.

I know the vice of envy. I know the grip of jealousy. I know that she's just a normal little girl who loves to excel and achieve. And I know it's hard to watch her little brother be first.

I know we're going to be happy about the highs in our family and mourn together in the lows, even when they are at the same time. That is what we're about.

Romans 12:15

Rejoice with those who rejoice; mourn with those who mourn.

Prayer

Father, thank you for my family. Teach us to be thankful for the good seasons, for the blessings of others. Help us rejoice in the victories of one another and to build one another up. Give me wisdom in bringing out the best in my children. Amen.

17

The Sound You Hear

Dinner at our house is wild. It's loud. It's messy. It's crazy. Sometimes our toddler refuses to eat a bite. Our daughter shakes ketchup everywhere but on her plate. Our son spills his apple juice, and someone bursts into tears (and it's not always a child).

There are noodles on the floor, kids getting up and down, and conversation without limits. If you listened, you might hear whining, crying, laughing, talking, smacking, chomping, and chewing.

I used to get so frustrated during dinnertime. I compared our noisy dinners to my picturesque idea of the perfect family dinner. But not too long ago it dawned on me to enjoy these boisterous, messy occasions, to laugh at the spills and capture the moment because I know I will look back on this time and miss it.

Plus, that perfect family? I've never met them, so they probably don't exist.

I do have some dining standards:

- Don't like what's on your plate? Try it. You might like it.
- Kids set the table and clean up the table.
- Play with your food (as long as you eat it, too).

- We don't miss dinner for playdates or TV time. We make eating together as a family a high priority.
- We don't lean back in our chairs, but if we do, we laugh if someone falls out.
- We can talk about anything at the table, as long as we respect one another and it doesn't make mom sick.

I can find many things at dinner I'd like to change. But I need to focus on the good and pick my battles: I love that we are together. I love that we have ample choices of food on our table. I love that I have the ability to clean it up (and that my hubby is a huge help). I love that my kids will try new foods.

And most of all, I love that the deafening sound I hear around the table is my family *living*.

Genesis 21:6

Sarah said, "God has brought me laughter, and everyone who hears about this will laugh with me."

Prayer

Jesus, thank you for my family. I love them so much, but they also break every rule in my book! Help me enjoy the children, the noise, the life that fills my home. I want to relish these moments, even when they are crazy! Amen.

18

I'm Not Going to Candy-Coat

It had been a very bad week.

It started off with my toddler and a staph infection. It was the fourth time someone in my family had contracted the deadly germ. (My parenting blog isn't called "We Are THAT Family" just for kicks.)

That same afternoon, my oldest returned from school looking pale. She was diagnosed with the flu the next morning in the same doctor's office. Our reputation preceded us.

I brought home $125 worth of Tamiflu for the entire family in an effort to keep the remaining soldiers well. My left eye is still twitching from writing that check.

My son, the healthy one, continued going to school. Toward the end of the week, I had run out of favors and actually had to pick him up from school. We stayed in our pajamas because it was going to be a quick trip.

That's when my car stalled in the car line, with one hundred cars behind me and in front of me (because I forgot that every time you wear your pajamas in public, your car quits).

I think I handled the mortifying moment in stride: with the toddler on my hip and my flu-ridden, embarrassed girl on the sidewalk, I directed traffic around my broken-down car.

My mom pulled up (after a quick, desperate call), rolled down her window, and said, "You really are THAT family."

I wasn't about to argue with my only ride home. Plus, my mom is a smart lady. My hubby rescued my car. He was happy to report that I had just run out of gas. Surprisingly, this did not make me feel better.

Let's face it: moms have a hard job and some weeks (or months, lo, years) are bad. Everything goes wrong, and we just have to deal. I think the Bible calls them trials. God allows them to develop perseverance in us. He teaches us patience and dependence on him.

He even tells us to count it as joy when we face trials. (I think this means it's OK to throw your hands in the air and laugh, even while wearing your pajamas in public.)

James 1:2-4

Consider it pure joy, my brothers, whenever you face trials of many kinds, because you know that the testing of your faith develops perseverance. Perseverance must finish its work so that you may be mature and complete, not lacking anything.

Prayer

Jesus, when life gets hard and things go wrong, I usually just want to complain and grumble. Please remind me that these hard times develop something in me that I need for this journey: faith and perseverance. Amen.

19

The Best Mom

I felt frumpy the other day. Tired, worn out, and just unattractive and overworked.

A tornado of children and dirt had blown through my home. My hair needed some serious color care. My pants were tight, and my eyebrows, toes, and house needed some professional help.

I felt it on the inside, too, all the way down to my bones. I felt like I was trying to keep all the plates spinning at the same time. I was doing everything I normally did—balancing home, kids, hubby, part-time job—but none of it excellently. It was just one foot in front of the other, one day down, a thousand to go.

In the middle of my pity party, my son crawled into my lap, all gangly elbows and knees pushing into me. I was finishing up some mundane mother-task when he leaned in and said, "You're the best mother I've ever had."

Immediately I was tempted to laugh it off: "How many mothers have you had?" or "Oh, yeah, folding laundry makes me mother of the year!" As I started to tease him, something stopped me.

It was the look in his eyes. When I looked deeply, I could see his heart in his big eyes. Oh my. He meant it.

And so, I said two words. The two right words: "Thank you."

He hugged me and ran off, unaware of the torrent of emotions he'd just unleashed. Nothing could have snapped me out of frumpiness except a moment like that: one of pure love.

I'm the only mother he's had, so thankfully, the comparisons are few. But I'm the mother my children are supposed to have. They love me in all my frumpiness. Am I the best mom? No. But I'm their mom, good and bad.

And that's enough.

 ## Proverbs 6:20-22

My son, keep your father's commandment,
 and forsake not your mother's teaching.
Bind them on your heart always;
 tie them around your neck.
When you walk, they will lead you;
 when you lie down, they will watch over you;
and when you awake, they will talk with you.
(English Standard Version)

 ## Prayer

God, my job is so big and my responsibilities are great. I grow tired in all that I do. My kids don't care how much money is in the bank or how clean the house is; they just want me. They are learning from what I do. Help me teach them well. Amen.

20

Her Life Is Better Than Mine

I have a friend who lives in an amazing house, has well-behaved children, and has more than enough money for every need and want. Oh, and she's beautiful. And if all that isn't enough, she's a wonderful person, who gives to the poor, defends the weak, serves others. She has an amazing life.

I used to think it was better than mine.

You don't have to be a genius to realize that some people have more than you. You only have to be *human*.

It's in our nature to compare our bodies, our hair, our homes, our mothering to others. I wish I had a bigger _____, more _____ like her. Women compare. We compete. We covet.

And we grieve God when we do.

The cost of comparison is high. When I compared myself to my friend, it only magnified my own insecurities. It only left me feeling discouraged. It created a desire in me to be something other than I am.

There is only one me. I wasn't designed to look like or act like or be like my friend. God created her, called her to something. I have my own job. He gave me my children. He created their spirited personalities for me to mother.

Comparison to others affects our motives. It changes how we live our lives for the wrong reasons.

As believers, we're all in a race. But in our mind-set, a race signifies a competition, one against another. But we aren't competing against other believers for the prize. We are running toward the prize of Jesus. There isn't a trophy podium for first, second, and third place. We are all first-place winners by finishing the race.

I'm never going to have a house like my friend's, and my kids don't have the quiet personalities of hers. And no matter how much I try, I'll never have her body (insert another cupcake here). But that's OK. I'm not supposed to.

It turns out that her life isn't really better than mine. It's just hers. I wouldn't trade our lives for anything.

Galatians 5:24-26

Those who belong to Christ Jesus have crucified the sinful nature with its passions and desires. Since we live by the Spirit, let us keep in step with the Spirit. Let us not become conceited, provoking and envying each other.

Prayer

Jesus, I just want to thank you for all that you've given me: my family, my friends, my home, and my life. I don't want to compare myself to others. It's not pleasing to you, and it makes me feel ungrateful. Thank you for the many gifts you've given me. Amen.

2 1

The Unwritten Script

I spent nearly the first ten years of my marriage working at churches with my husband.

It was a full decade of good and bad.

Our last staff position was full of pain, confusion, and failure. Our dream job turned into a nightmare. We were isolated across the country from friends and family: anxiety became our companion and fear our partner.

It's been several years since we made the decision to quit that job, sell our home, and move close to family. It was our greatest leap of faith.

We lived without a job in a borrowed home for six months. It was a scary time but is now one of my most treasured seasons.

During those months, we struggled with our identity, but we healed. It was a slow process, but we realized God had not forgotten us.

I like to think I'm over it.

And then when I least expect it, there it is—when God doesn't make sense in the unanswered and often unspoken questions we all have in the unwritten script of our lives.

Life is about free choice. We all have the power of choice. And we love this! I love the freedom to decide for myself. I would never give it away.

But when I think of my children having free choice, to decide whatever they want, I'm not quite as confident in this great freedom. I like control. I like freedom for me but not for everyone else.

I can't control what others choose. I can't stop the poor choices my kids might make, or worse, the choices of an evil person. I can't have my free choice but not allow it for others.

That's why our lives are unscripted. God knows what we will choose, but he lets us choose. And sometimes those choices aren't the best.

God allows pain into our lives because he is more concerned with our character than with our comfort or convenience. He can take man's poor choices and rewrite the script of our lives.

It is God's mystery.

And we have a choice: we can kick and scream our way through a difficult situation, or we can say God is in this. He is good. We can see him in the midst of our pain and in the script of our lives.

Proverbs 16:9

In his heart a man plans his course,
　　but the LORD determines his steps.

Prayer

Father, thank you for loving me enough to give me the choice to love you in return. Help me not go off on my own diversions, away from the path you've set my feet on. Lead me, Lord, in your ways. Amen.

22

Slowing Down So We Can Keep Up

I had a bit of a meltdown. I really did. I woke up one day and decided I couldn't do it anymore. For months, I'd been feeling stressed about our schedule and the demands on our time. I was spending hours every week dropping my kids off at extracurricular activities after school. We would eat a rushed dinner and hurry off to bath and bed.

Now, I know the car shuffling is a normal mom activity, but seriously, my kids were eight, six, and one at the time. Did they really need to master every sport? Wasn't there plenty of time for those things in junior high and high school? I had heard that in our town, just to make a team sport in public school, you have to be an expert by the time you're seven.

Instead of keeping up, I decided maybe we should just move.

The plethora of activities offered on a silver platter to children in our society boggles my mind. Am I a bad mom because I didn't have my daughter in tumbling lessons so she could be cheerleader one day? Does my toddler really need Spanish lessons to get into college?

So, I just stopped it all. We decided to put everything on hold. We decided to slow our lives down so that we could keep up with our kids' lives instead of everyone else's. Do you know how my kids reacted? They were relieved.

I know my kids will develop individual passions, but it's hard to home in on that when there's so much noise. We decided to be intentional with our extra time, like volunteering as a family, giving to others, and just being home together.

I didn't realize how hard I was trying to be like everyone else until I stopped. I was conforming to the demands of a world that doesn't always have my children's best interests in mind.

The change has been remarkable. It's refreshing to be more intentional with our time. I see a big difference in my kids. I feel a big difference in me.

John 15:19

If you belonged to the world, it would love you as its own. As it is, you do not belong to the world, but I have chosen you out of the world. That is why the world hates you.

Prayer

God, I praise you for your grace. It sustains me. Thank you for showing me that my desire to be like everyone else is wrong. Help me conform to you and not to the world around me. Amen.

2 3

One Day My Prince Will Come

Cinderella. She's a big deal at our house. I'm serious. The kids like her, too.

She is *the* princess to love. And why wouldn't she be? Her story begins as a broken, unloved girl, dressed badly. She gets help from some talking mice and the supernatural, has a major transformation, gets the cute guy, and lives happily ever after. It's all very realistic.

I'll never forget the day my firstborn met Cinderella. She was two. We lived in Florida and scored tickets to Disney World by listening to a two-hour time-share presentation. (Those were the good old days.) At ten years old, my daughter still remembers that moment when she flew into the princess's arms. Dreams do come true.

I'll never forget it either. We waited in line for an hour. We were hot, sweaty, and tired. But my eyes filled with tears as I watched my baby run into Cinderella's waiting arms. My hubby looked at me and then at Cinderella and said, "Maybe she is real." And y'all, I think he meant it.

When I think of my life—the bad choices I've made, the grace I've been given, the miracle that I call my children—I can't help feeling like my little girl did when she met Cinderella for the first time.

One day I will run into my father's arms. I will meet the one who gave me life and made me a mother. Our world teaches little girls that a prince will come. They are right, but he will arrive in the sky on a horse and take us with him to heaven. It will be a dream come true.

It will be very realistic.

John 14:1-3

Do not let your hearts be troubled. Trust in God; trust also in me. In my Father's house are many rooms; if it were not so, I would have told you. I am going there to prepare a place for you. And if I go and prepare a place for you, I will come back and take you to be with me that you also may be where I am.

Prayer

Jesus, thank you for making a home for me in heaven. I know it's real, but I get so caught up in my life here on earth. Help me remember that my heavenly home isn't a fairy tale. I long to meet my prince. Amen.

2 4

Turned Off

Simplify. It's a simple word with powerful implications.

I'm not talking about eating homegrown food from my nonexistent garden and hand-sewing all my children's clothes—because that would leave us hungry and naked.

I'm talking about a deep desire to slow down, to parent our children intentionally, and to make every day count.

Since becoming parents a decade ago, we have worked hard teaching morality and character. We've gone to church and even memorized a handful of Scriptures. We've tried.

But do you know who has tried harder to teach our kids? The media.

Now, I'm not against TV, movies, and music. I think there are some great preschool shows that help with numbers and colors out there. We enjoy family movie night a couple of times a month, and occasionally we splurge and go to the movies together.

But I am against bad TV and the mindless, senseless prattle that is offered in huge doses to my kids. When I was a kid at least there was *Little House on the Prairie* and *Happy Days*. We could find bits of value, even from Fonzie.

Today, kids are inundated with junk. I'll be the first to admit, we subscribed fully. We turned them loose with the kids' programming for a couple of hours a day after their homework was completed. It didn't take long to discover that just because it says DISNEY doesn't mean it has VALUE.

Two years ago, we noticed that our son could quote entirely too much of the garbage. It was a huge wake-up call. It was disheartening to discover so much bad media geared toward kids. But it was even more heart-breaking that we allowed it.

We are turned off by it, so we turned it off. We didn't get rid of the television or dump our Disney movie collection; we're just more involved. We know everything they watch, when they are allowed. We limited all combined screen time (computers, video games, TV) to thirty minutes during the week.

We now fill those empty hours with more meaningful activities, and we don't even miss the strong influence of the media in our home!

There is a strong pull toward the world and the things in it. Our job as parents is to dig in our heels and fight against the pull. Jesus has asked that we be holy as he is, set apart from the world, turned off by the un-godliness we see in our society. It's a daily choice and sometimes we fail, but we are making strides to honor him in our home.

2 Timothy 2:21-22

If a man cleanses himself from the latter [ignoble purposes], he will be an instrument for noble purposes, made holy, useful to the Master and prepared to do any good work. Flee the evil desires of youth, and pursue righteousness, faith, love and peace, along with those who call on the Lord out of a pure heart.

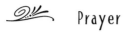 ## Prayer

Jesus, I know I'm in the world but not of this world. The pull of the world is so strong. Help me resist it for myself and show my children that we are to pursue righteousness, not worldliness. Amen.

2 5

Playing Church

I tossed my three-year-old girl in the tub with her big sister the other night. (I asked permission from my oldest first. She still has a lot of little girl left in her and welcomed the toys. And I didn't actually toss my toddler.)

They played and splashed, and I went to the kitchen for just a minute, until I heard my youngest crying.

I hurried back in to find my oldest BEAMING and my youngest sniffling.

"What happened?" I asked as I mopped up the tub water from the floor.

"Mom, guess what," my oldest said in a very excited voice. "I helped her ask Jesus into her heart! She repeated a prayer after me!"

"Wow! Honey, that's great. I'm so proud of you for doing that," I said, watching my toddler nod her head in agreement, with a giant tear rolling down her cheek. "But why is she crying?"

"Oh, well, I also baptized her."

I laughed as I dried my little girl's face and rolled my eyes at my oldest daughter's antics. This wasn't the first time they had played church. It always warms my heart when they mimic what they see.

I looked at the faces of my daughters and felt such a longing for them to know Jesus. Not just of him and the things we do in church but truly fellowship with the one who died for them.

I want Jesus to be their best friend. I want them to ask his advice before mine. I want them to share their burdens and hurts, dreams and longings with Jesus. I long for my girls to find their security and esteem in the God who created them in his image.

I want them to find what I have in him. But even now, I sometimes catch *myself* playing church. Tuning out instead of tuning in, getting pulled back into my selfishness, losing perspective.

Then I remember those little girls are mimicking what they see. If they see me just "playing church," they will, too. It's one game I don't want us to play.

Mark 10:15

I tell you the truth, anyone who will not receive the kingdom of God like a little child will never enter it.

Prayer

Little hands are mimicking mine. Little feet are following behind. Jesus, help me walk straight, not waver to the left or right. I want to lead my children to you. Amen.

2 6

When My Children Teach Me

My daughters have strong, determined personalities. They do not give up! They fight for what they believe in and don't care what other people think. If my older girl catches me looking around to gauge what others are thinking of our latest fiasco, she says, "Mom, who cares if people are staring?" (Sometimes we are stare-worthy!)

Her self-confidence builds up my own.

My son has a gift, too: He makes friends with the friendless. He seeks out the loner, the child who is different, the one who needs a friend.

The principal of our elementary school actually awarded him for his compassion. At the time, I didn't know the story behind the honor.

He befriended a special-needs boy and became his personal guide. The teachers were touched by his selfless act and honored him for it. I asked him about it the other day: "What is it about this boy that made you want to be his friend?"

"Well. He smiles all the time. He's always happy, but he learns different and is loud sometimes. He needed extra help, and I'm good at that. Plus, I needed a friend, too," he said with a shrug.

My oldest daughter said, "Does he have Down syndrome?" (One of her dearest friends has Down syndrome.)

"No," he said and scrunched up his face, a bit confused by his sister's question. "I think he has Up syndrome. He's always happy."

[Please note: I took the opportunity to encourage my kids to continue to love and accept children with special needs. I believe this is a conversation every parent must have.]

Syndrome or not, it doesn't matter; he saw a boy who needed a friend and knew that was something he was really good at. My son has taught me about friendship. Everyone needs a friend and everyone can be a friend.

Matthew 18:1-4

At that time the disciples came to Jesus, saying, "Who is the greatest in the kingdom of heaven?" And calling to him a child, he put him in the midst of them and said, "Truly, I say to you, unless you turn and become like children, you will never enter the kingdom of heaven. Whoever humbles himself like this child is the greatest in the kingdom of heaven." (English Standard Version)

Prayer

Sweet Jesus, thank you for loving children and for not turning them away. They are precious gifts, and often they hear your words in their hearts quicker than I do. Please help me learn from the children you've given me. Amen.

27

Go Ask Your Dad

As I stirred the spaghetti sauce, I carefully replaced the lid and leaned over the sink to wash off the spoon. This simple task was made especially difficult because I had a toddler attached to both my legs. She was making pitiful sounds that sounded something like HOLD ME, MOMMY!

I pried her loose, scooped her up, and went to the kitchen table where my big kids were doing homework. I answered a few questions from my son and sat down to help my fourth grader with math. MATH! (Not my strongest suit.) My toddler was finally distracted enough to get down, and I reread the math word problem again, as if that would help.

"Mom, that is not right. You don't understand it, do you?" my daughter asked in a tone that made me feel like a real genius. "Ask your dad when he gets home," I said.

I returned to the stove and bubbling-over noodle water. Ugh. How can I actually burn spaghetti noodles? I silently scolded myself. As I was cleaning off the burners, my toddler wandered back into the kitchen.

"Mommy, I sorry," she said in a soft voice.

"Why, honey?" I asked without looking up from my scrubbing.

"I sorry for coloring on the wall. With markers."

And at the same time:

"Mom, can I have a snack?"

"M-o-o-o-m, I need help with this math!"

My hubby walked through the door—at the same time all three of my kids needed me.

I screamed, "GO ASK YOUR DAD!" I retreated to my bathroom and turned on the tub. I closed my eyes to stop the tears I could feel welling up.

As I soaked away my worries and left my hubby to do *my* job, I reflected and tried to reassure myself. *It was just a hard day. I don't lose it very often. I can do this. I am a good mom.*

I told my kids to "Go ask your dad" because we all knew he could help. He could answer tricky math problems. He wouldn't mind offering a snack or wiping away washable markers. Most of all, he would take up where I left off because we're a team, and he's on my side.

It was at that moment that I turned to *my* dad. Not my earthly father miles away, but my heavenly father, who was right there with me. I cried and asked for strength, wisdom, and an extra large dose of patience.

I decided right then, I would lean on my father in heaven as much as I lean on my kids' father.

James 1:17

Every good and perfect gift is from above, coming down from the Father of the heavenly lights, who does not change like shifting shadows.

Prayer

Dear Father, I am your child and I know you love me. Some days I try too hard to do things on my own, and I end up frustrated, and I fail. Help me lean on you. You're my dad—you have good gifts for me and I need your help. Amen.

28

The Path of Least Resistance

We were heading home from church as the rain poured. Large raindrops danced on the windshield.

My observant daughter asked, "Dad, why do the raindrops go straight down and then stop and move in another direction?"

I watched the rain do just as she said. (I'm so glad she asked her dad this question.)

"Well, honey, it's called the path of least resistance." And then he said something exactly like, "The path of least resistance describes the physical or metaphorical pathway that provides the least resistance to forward motion by a given object or entity, among a set of alternative paths. The concept is often used to describe why an object or entity takes a given path." Only I had to copy and paste that from Wikipedia because I don't do science.

They continued in a deep, meaningful conversation about the metaphorical pathways as I daydreamed (not unlike in my old science classes of yore).

The Path of Least Resistance and I know each other well. As a parent, I'm often drawn down the easy road. It is an uncomplicated path; it makes everyone happy. There aren't obstacles or challenges. Nothing stands in the way on this road.

It's easier to give in to our kids than to offer resistance. It's quieter; there's less drama and tears. But this isn't the road God wants us to travel. He gives us the strength to parent well, to ask for obedience, to follow through with appropriate consequences for bad behavior. God gives us the courage to parent our precious gifts on the correct path, even if there is some resistance.

I will warn you. It's not a popular road. It goes against the flow. It's hard and not for the fainthearted, but if parenting is our job, then we must do it well.

"I don't like the path of least resistance!" I blurted in the car that day.

My daughter and husband looked at me strangely, but I resolved in my heart to be strong and to not give in to pressures to follow the popular path. It's easy to be like everyone else; it's hard to stand alone. My kids dislike correction the same as everyone else, but I've learned that if I'm doing my job the way God wants me to, I'm more concerned about the path they're on and not their immediate happiness.

Matthew 7:13-14

Enter through the narrow gate. For wide is the gate and broad is the road that leads to destruction, and many enter through it. But small is the gate and narrow the road that leads to life, and only a few find it.

Prayer

Father, I want to parent in a godly manner. I want to lead my kids down the narrow road. Some days, it's just easier to give in to their demands or just do what everyone else is doing. Help me be strong. Please give me wisdom to make good choices. Amen.

2 9

Raising Little Women

I searched everywhere: every single drawer in my bathroom (mental note: those need to be cleaned), under the cabinets, and in random places like the tub and even the refrigerator. I couldn't find my hairbrush anywhere!

Running late, frustration mounting, I yelled "Girls!" Only it sounded more like "GIIIRRRRLLLLLLSSSS!"

They both appeared at the doorway looking guilty before I had even accused them. "Where is my brush? Have you seen it?"

"No," they answered in unison. My oldest declared, "We haven't touched it."

I grumbled under my breath and stomped upstairs to their bathroom. There it sat on the counter.

I grabbed it, but before I could begin my verbal assault, I was taken back twenty-something years to another bathroom, another mother, and another daughter, *me*.

The same argument occurred on a regular basis in my childhood home. My mom always carefully placed her hair pick (it was the 1980s, and we sported home permanents) in the same place. But weekly, almost as if it were planned, my twin sister and I were summoned to find a missing pick.

We are all grown up now, raising two daughters each ourselves.

As I grabbed my brush, appointment forgotten, I decided to forgo the lecture. It seemed a battle unworthy of the fight. Somewhere between looking for and finding that silly hairbrush, it dawned on me that I have a heavy task before me. The memory from my past clashed with the present moment, and I recalled that just like my mom, I'm raising little women.

Oh, sure, I'd thought about it before. But the weight of the moment was heavy. My girls were complicated, strong-willed, demanding at times, and dramatic. A lot like me, actually.

I'm my mother's age when I thought she was old. My oldest is halfway grown, with a little sister in her footsteps. Time passes so quickly, and my time with them will quickly turn from authority to influence.

I don't know how to grow their confidence, bolster their self-esteem. I'm not sure how to help them value their inner beauty more than their outer. I don't have the magic words to make them strong when their world crumbles around them. But I do know I can't do it alone.

With God's help, I pray for them in the dark of the night, whispering over them. With God's help, I guide them into maturity and follow his leading. With God's help, I can raise my little women.

 Proverbs 22:6

Train a child in the way he should go,
    and when he is old he will not turn from it.

Prayer

Heavenly Father, you love my children even more than I do. You want them to follow you even more than I want them to. Parenting can be so frustrating, and some days I just don't know what to do. Please grant me wisdom. Amen.

30

He Will Be Someone's Husband Someday

Iwanted to throw the remote control at the television. If it delivered news of another man cheating on his wife, I would scream! I turned it off before the box had a chance to disappoint me again and said aloud, "What is wrong with men? They are such jerks!"

I noticed my seven-year-old son standing in the doorway just in time to hear me. The confused look on his face made my heart ache, and my harsh words made me want to bite my tongue. "Except for you, honey, and Daddy," I said as I hugged him.

He returned to what he was doing, seemingly unbothered by my words.

But I didn't escape them so easily.

That beautiful brown-eyed boy in the other room, who stole my heart the minute I met him, will be someone's husband someday. I had not only stereotyped an entire gender but also lumped my own precious men into the mix.

I don't know what makes husbands cheat, or wives for that matter. Maybe it isn't any one thing. All I know is that I want to teach my son to value women, to respect his sisters, to honor them with his actions as a young boy and as a mature man.

I'm pretty sure this doesn't happen just because I wish it. My son is watching how his daddy treats me. He's learning by the way I speak to my spouse. Our home is the classroom, we are the teachers, and it turns out our kids are pretty perceptive students.

If we don't teach them how to act, someone else will.

I asked God that day to help me lead my children in how I want them to treat their future mates, and I prayed for them wherever they might be.

Deuteronomy 4:9

Only be careful, and watch yourselves closely so that you do not forget the things your eyes have seen or let them slip from your heart as long as you live. Teach them to your children and to their children after them.

Prayer

Dear Lord, what a big responsibility you've given me! It's an honor to raise children. It's a blessing. But it's not easy. I get caught up in the moment and sometimes forget that I'm to teach my children by leading them. They watch me, follow me, and help me not to stumble. But when I do, give me the courage to admit it, learn from it, get up, and try again. Amen.

3 1

I Lost My Pride in Walmart

Do you have days that are etched into your heart and mind? You know, the kind that warm your heart, like being called "mommy" the first time, first steps, graduations, achievements, and so on?

I do, too. On especially hard days, I like to think about those moments and remember that I'm a good mom and that my kids are pretty wonderful.

I will never forget the day I lost my pride in Walmart, of all places. (Don't judge me; I know you've had superstore moments yourself.) I was chasing my four-year-old daughter and dragging my two-year-old son to the bathroom. They didn't need to "go." I did. (And if you have a "mom bladder," this needs no further explanation.)

Once we were finally in the stall, I bolted the door and proceeded with quite an interested audience. As I threatened my daughter to *leave the door locked* while I was in such an unbecoming position, my son was staring at me.

"Mommy! Mommy!" he yelled in his clear, loud voice.

"What, honey?" I whispered back in my own exasperated one.

"YOU DON'T HAVE A *PENIS*," he said in astonishment. (And this was said as loudly and clearly as humanly possible, and in slow motion.)

I didn't breathe for a full ninety seconds. You could have heard a pin drop. The whispering and talking outside the stall ceased. I mentally kicked myself for teaching him the "proper" body part names and re-minded myself to burn that parenting book once I got home.

Then I heard laughing.

We stayed in that stall for a very long time.

Of all my premothering dreams, this was not one of them. I was deeply embarrassed. But I left my wounded pride in the bathroom that day. It was just the beginning of many lessons to come.

God has a unique way of using our own offspring to teach us valuable lessons. As a matter of fact, most of what I've learned about God and my-self has been through them. He has taught me humility in some of the most embarrassing situations. It's been good for me.

I was an awesome mother until I had kids. Now, I'm just like everyone else.

Proverbs 11:2

When pride comes, then comes disgrace,
but with humility comes wisdom.

Prayer

Thank you, God, for making me a mother. It's the hardest and best job I've ever had. Thank you for teaching me the hard lessons and for humbling me. It's in those raw moments that you offer the wisdom I need so badly. Help me learn these lessons well, so I don't have to repeat them often. Amen.

3 2

Letting Go of Your Child

Her tiny body, delivered weeks too early, was strapped to the bed in the Neonatal Intensive Care Unit. She was struggling to maintain her body temperature and I my composure.

It was Christmas Eve, and our third baby, not due until February, was fighting for her life. We rushed to the hospital, leaving my mother to watch over our other children at home, while my father stood next to my premature baby. He did what my hubby and I couldn't do. He prayed. Our silent tears mixed, and we asked God for a miracle.

It was a surreal moment I'll remember forever. In that moment of complete desperation, nothing else mattered. It was life versus death. It was the day I let go of my baby. It was the day God taught me how to trust.

This was her ninth day in the hospital. She had been getting better. I had been winning the battle for control since her surprise birth had spun control out of my hands. I had just held her recently for the first time and was going to try nursing the next day, and now this. She was again unstable and in crisis. In the silence, in *that* place, I let her go. I gave her back to God.

It was the most difficult decision I had ever made. I sobbed, "God, she is yours. You have only lent her to me. I give her back to you."

Suddenly, the monitors beeped, and all the eyes in the room tried to understand the numbers on the screen. She was stabilizing.

Eight days later, we brought our almost-five-pound girl home on a heart monitor. She stayed on it for five months. Today she is completely healthy.

I am reminded of Hannah, who gave Samuel, literally, back to God when he was about three years old. I cannot imagine this, no matter how hard I try. But I know that I will have to let go of my children one day. They will grow up and leave home.

Letting go is hard. It's unnatural in many ways. But it is necessary. Releasing them to God to fulfill their destiny is God's plan. In a way, we let go a little every day. Hannah had a thankful heart, even in the letting go.

1 Samuel 2:1-2

Then Hannah prayed and said:
"My heart rejoices in the LORD;
    in the LORD my horn is lifted high.
My mouth boasts over my enemies,
    for I delight in your deliverance.
"There is no one holy like the LORD;
    there is no one besides you;
    there is no Rock like our God."

Prayer

Jesus, my children are a gift. I am blessed to be their mother. But you are the gift giver. You made me a mother. My children are yours. As hard as it is, I offer them back to you. Help me in the letting go. Amen.

33

All By Myself

I dug in my heels and held on. It was an epic battle, and I was losing. I closed my eyes, took a deep breath, and pulled. Hard. I could smell victory, or maybe it was the coconut-scented lotion I was trying to pry from my toddler's hands.

"Give it to Mommy," I growled.

"No! I do it!" she wailed.

I lost my grip while she squeezed the bottle: a fountain of creamy scented lotion squirted high into the air.

It's hard to say who won the battle exactly. *But we both smelled pretty good.*

My daughter fought for control, to do things her way, because that's what toddlers do. It was a phase, but it was also developmental. Her desire for independence was natural and even good; it just needed to be channeled.

As a mother, I'm often the one to channel the energy and direct the wills of my children. It's a messy job.

I'm so much like her. But I'm grown and it's not a phase. When I stiffen my back, refuse to listen, and try to do it my way, it's anything but cute. I like to be in control. I'm the mom. I like for things to run my way. But there are times when I need to take my hands off, to let my kids fail, to let my husband make his own decisions, to let God be in control.

When I battle to do things *all by myself*, I don't win. I usually just end up with a mess. I am not designed to carry the weight of the world, or my small family for that matter. I can't fix every problem and prevent all hurts. I'm not supposed to.

I find that I'm much better at doing my job as nurturer and letting God do the rest.

Psalm 46:1-3, 7

God is our refuge and strength,

A very present help in trouble.

Therefore we will not fear,

Though the earth should change,

And though the mountains slip into the heart of the sea;

Though its waters roar and foam,

Though the mountains quake at its swelling pride. Selah. . . .

The LORD of hosts is with us;

The God of Jacob is our stronghold. (*New American Standard Bible*)

Prayer

Lord, I find myself struggling for control. My flesh wants to be in charge, but I don't want to be in a power struggle with you. Help me run to you as my refuge. Thank you for being my strength. I'm not meant to do life all by myself. Amen.

3 4

On Being a Mom and a Wife, Simultaneously

I curled up in bed, staring down at the babe nestled in the crook of my arm. How could one so small and young be so demanding? I'd only been a mother for six months. It was still so new to me, the responsibility, the ache to meet every need, the exhaustion from being needed so often.

I looked over at my husband deep in sleep. He needed me, too. Guilt clung to me like a heavy garment. I pushed him away the night before and said through frustrated tears, "Everyone wants something from me!" He nodded his head and turned away from me. His desire stifled another night, my heart empty.

Sometimes I'm exhausted from all the needing. The cup-filling, the feeding and cleaning, the reminding, and the redoing wear me out. Loving and doing are so rewarding but can be exhausting.

But it is also what makes me a mother.

My children will need me as long as they are children and I am mother. I want them to need me. But I also want my husband to want me. I want him to need me. It is the worn path of lovers. It's how we become mother, father, *and one*.

Pushing away the hazy fog and putting the baby in her own bed, I reached out to him.

It turns out *I needed him, too.*

Mothering can occupy the majority of our time, and our marriages can suffer in the wake of good intentions. We can be both caring mother and attentive wife, even when the needing is exhausting.

It is in those empty moments, when exhaustion clouds our minds and the needing is overwhelming, that we must turn to God. He can fill, refresh, and renew us with one word, one touch.

Because what children really need to see is Mom and Dad wanting each other.

1 Corinthians 7:5

Do not deprive each other except by mutual consent and for a time, so that you may devote yourselves to prayer. Then come together again so that Satan will not tempt you because of your lack of self-control.

Prayer

Father, thank you for the strength you give me to accomplish all that is set before me. Some days are so hard, and I just need your help. I cannot do it on my own. Help me love my spouse and my children as you love them. Amen.

3 5

Christmas Doesn't Have to End

I had put it off long enough: it was seven days after Christmas, and it was time to take down the decorations. The gifts had been put away (or, more likely, strewn over bedroom floors), the stockings were empty, and the tree, dripping with ornaments, was cockeyed.

I dragged empty containers into the family room and began to wrap special ornaments in paper to cradle them until next year. My toddler took in the scene and asked, "Whatcha doing, Mommy?"

"Well, Christmas is over and it's time to take down the tree. I'm just wrapping up the ornaments so they don't break," I explained.

Before I could blink, my little girl threw herself in front of the tree and stretched out her tiny arms to block my path, "Nooooo!" she screamed. "Not take away my tree. I love Christmas."

I stood there, surprised at her reaction as she fumbled some of her favorite ornaments off the tree and hid them under her shirt. I couldn't blame her, really. Christmas is for kids—the bright lights and colors, the Santa lore, the new toys.

"Honey, Christmas is over. It's time to put these things away," I gently said.

She ran and grabbed baby Jesus from the manger and held him to her heart.

And that's when it hit me: Christmas isn't over. It never ends. It's not about the gifts and décor. "Oh, honey, I'm sorry. It's time to put away the tree, but baby Jesus can stay with us all year."

Christmas is about Jesus. But I don't want Jesus to be about Christmas. I want him in my home every day of the year. I want visitors to see some evidence of the Christ child not only in my life but also in my home. I don't want to remember him only for the holiday season that too often forgets him. I don't ever want Christmas to end.

It took a three-year-old to remind me that it doesn't have to.

Galatians 2:20

I have been crucified with Christ and I no longer live, but Christ lives in me. The life I live in the body, I live by faith in the Son of God, who loved me and gave himself for me.

Prayer

Jesus, thank you for coming to this earth and taking on humanity. You made the ultimate sacrifice so that we can celebrate your presence every day. Thank you for giving yourself up for me so that I can have new life in you. Amen.

36

Losing Control

I am a very careful person. I always wear my seatbelt. I like to follow the rules. I wouldn't dream of removing the DO NOT REMOVE tag from my pillows, because whoever did never lived to tell the story. I'm just sure of it.

I married my polar opposite. And then we had children. Guess which genes are stronger. I think the accident-prone ones are dominant.

All three of my kids have had stitches and CAT scans. We usually meet our annual deductible in January. So, that should give you an idea.

The other day, my older daughter found the crutches.

My son once used the only five-dollar bill he had to his name to buy a pair of crutches at a thrift store. You know, because he doesn't have toys. Soon after, he fell down the stairs while using them. I put them away because I just can't bear the irony of my children breaking bones while playing on crutches.

Having discovered my hiding place, my daughter was goofing off with said crutches, and I told her to go put them back upstairs. She obeyed immediately.

I guess I should have told her to carefully put them away. She carried them over her head and hit the light fixture on the stairwell, which resulted in *shattered glass everywhere*.

Some days, I just can't win.

I think God likes to keep me in that place. Do you know the one? The place where I have to step back and pull my hands away because it's not in my control. I like order. I like things to run smoothly, my way. I like to be in control.

But I'm not. My efforts are in vain. I can't make the sun shine on a rainy day. I can't make my kids behave all the time, everywhere. I can't because I'm not supposed to.

There is one who spoke and the earth was formed. There is one who calms the raging storm and quiets the fierce winds. He is in control. He is not surprised by my dilemmas or fearful of the unknown. Sometimes he lets us have our way so he can show up.

Matthew 8:26-27

[Jesus] replied, "You of little faith, why are you so afraid?" Then he got up and rebuked the winds and the waves, and it was completely calm. The men were amazed and asked, "What kind of man is this? Even the winds and the waves obey him!"

Prayer

Jesus, I know that you are in control of my life. I make a mess of things most of the time. I want you to quiet the storms in my life and help me remember to loosen my control and turn it over to you. Amen.

3 7

Fitting Africa into My
American-Shaped Heart

In the spring of 2010, I traveled to Africa with Compassion International to blog about their relief efforts. I went to change the world. Instead, the trip rocked mine.

I saw Jesus in the slums. I felt his hand when an orphaned girl grabbed mine. I recognized him in the dirt-stained face of a widow who had taken in four orphaned children. I caught a glimpse of his holiness as I watched a child with disabilities dance before her Lord. I had to look away from such undefiled purity.

I walked down a filthy path surrounded by images I can't describe: depravity, extreme poverty, and gut-wrenching hopelessness. My senses were overwhelmed as silent tears coursed down my cheeks. But the road led me to Jesus. In this desolate place, I saw joy, unspeakable and full of glory.

I met children who knew Jesus and for whom that was more than enough. He offered them a hope and a future that were impossible to find in their surroundings.

The irony struck me hard: joy in a place that mirrors hell. I couldn't help thinking of my cushy home in an American suburb. In my country, my town, *my own life*, where I have everything I need and so much of what I want. But joy is hard to find. I often equate things and circumstances with my level of joy.

Joy is delighting in good things that satisfy. The people I met were joyful because they had found something exceptionally good and satisfying. God had quenched their hunger, satisfied them.

I returned home, back to my life. But I long to be like the poor. I crave for my hunger to be satisfied by God and by him alone. Life as I have known it is ruined, and I wouldn't have it any other way.

 ## Psalm 69:32-33

The poor will see and be glad—
    you who seek God, may your hearts live!
The LORD hears the needy
    and does not despise his captive people.

Prayer

Jesus, you have given me so much. I look around at my life and recognize that even though I might have needs, I have a place to sleep. I have food and clean water. Please remind me of these many blessings when I feel like my life is lacking. Help me remember that only you can satisfy the deep hunger in my heart. Amen.

3 8

The Disease

Right before bedtime, my pajama-clad son hurried to my room with his shirt sleeve pulled back. I saw that my husband was tending to his arm, so I continued what I was doing.

Then I heard my husband's voice. "Hon, you need to look at this."

Insert psycho mom here: I am a worrier. I'm an obsessive googler of all things medical concerning my kiddos. It's a sickness, really.

My hand froze because I knew that tone. The one that (very calmly) says, *Get over here right now because you're going to want to google this strange sickness.*

Or something like that.

I grabbed my son's arm and gasped at the ugly, red, splotchy, rash-type thing on the inside of his forearm. Questions ensued: "Did you fall?" "Does it hurt?" "Honey, does it look like it's swelling?" "Did a spider bite you?"

He shook his head and looked a little scared. "I'm sure it's OK," I told him, hiding my inward panic. "We'll just keep an eye on it," and I hugged him off to bed.

I'm not going to lie. Google is *not* my friend.

I slept The Worried Mom Sleep (which is also known as *not at all*).

The next morning, his bruise looked the same, only a darker red. I pushed the skin around, but he didn't complain and ran off to play.

Maybe this is just one of those unknowns, I thought.

While I was blow-drying my hair, my son sauntered in. I turned off the dryer. "Did you need something?"

"No, I was just looking for my car. Oh, by the way, I think I know what happened to my arm."

"What?"

"Well, I don't know if this is it or not, but yesterday I sucked on my arm."

"Excuse me?"

"I wanted to see what would happen. I just remembered."

My son's rare disease: a self-induced hickey.

I breathed a sigh of relief, but only after I said, "WE DO NOT SUCK ON OUR SKIN UNTIL IT BRUISES." I added that to the list entitled "1,000 Things I Never Thought I'd Say to My Kids."

As I was thinking about it later (and, yes, laughing to myself), I thought how often I get myself in similar situations. I rush through the day without reading my Bible, without praying, without making my relationship with God a priority. Then, I look for reasons for my grumpiness, my impatience, and my "rash" of bad behavior. I might even blame it on others or the unknown.

When I am honest with myself, it doesn't take long for me to remember that *I'm* the cause of my current "illness." I have a bad attitude, a short temper, because I did it to myself. In other words, sometimes I suck. (Sorry, couldn't resist!)

Psalm 105:1-4

Give thanks to the LORD, call on his name;

make known among the nations what he has done.

Sing to him, sing praise to him;

tell of all his wonderful acts.

Glory in his holy name;

let the hearts of those who seek the LORD rejoice.

Look to the LORD and his strength;

seek his face always.

 Prayer

Lord, sometimes I am my own worst enemy. I get caught up in the busyness of life, and I forget to make you a part of my day. Please forgive me and help me make my relationship with you a priority. Amen.

3 9

Trying to Change Things I Can't

As we pulled into the driveway, I heaved a sigh of relief: we were home. It had been a good trip visiting family, but the drive had been long and hard.

We lugged heavy suitcases, tired bodies, and empty snack bags to the front door. As soon as we opened the door, I knew something was wrong.

Hint: My house smelled. Bad.

We dropped our load in the entryway and dispersed throughout the house. A piercing scream erupted from upstairs. My daughter found the problem: she had accidentally closed our cat in her bedroom for nearly *four days*.

Thankfully, our thoughtful cat decided my daughter's double bed could double as a litter box (because a mattress is cheaper than new carpet). But, still, it was disgusting and horrifying and not funny at all.

I ranted: "How did the cat get locked up? Mercy, what will we do? Mattresses are expensive!" and on and on with the what-ifs and oh-mys.

At one point, my hubby looked at me and said, "It's done. We can't do anything about it. We'll just learn from this, clean up the mess, and move on."

So, that's what we did.

But his wise words stuck with me. Why do I try so hard to change the things I can't? I waste time complaining about things that have already happened, things I can't change. I worry and fret and overthink and *change nothing*.

I cry over spilled milk. Not literally (unless the spilled milk is on carpet).

As a mom, I dedicate a lot of time to trying to change things I can't: spills and messes and behavior gone wrong. It dawned on me (too late) that every negative word I uttered about the cat incident hurt my daughter.

God, my father, has seen some of the messes I've created (some accidents, some not), but rather than berate me for what's already occurred, he forgives and forgets the offense and gives me a fresh start.

He doesn't remind me of my past mistakes; he offers a future and hope.

He changes the things we can't: us.

Ephesians 4:22-24

You were taught, with regard to your former way of life, to put off your old self, which is being corrupted by its deceitful desires; to be made new in the attitude of your minds; and to put on the new self, created to be like God in true righteousness and holiness.

Prayer

Heavenly Father, I spend a lot of time trying to change circumstances I can't. I worry and fret and waste my time doing so. Please help me trust you. I give you my past, all my mistakes. I offer you my future and ask that you make me more like you. Amen.

4 0

Our Father

After school, many of the children stay and play on the playground. They are bursting with energy, and it's a great time for mothers to gather 'round and catch up.

And so it was on an average day. I was trying to keep an eye on my toddler as she weaved in and out among the "big kids." I was also talking to a couple of friends. I saw one of them look behind me and heard her gasp and whisper my son's name.

My heart started pounding before I could even turn around. When I did, I saw a huge man carrying my seven-year-old son like a baby. My son's face was red, streaked with dirt and tears. I didn't know the stranger who carried my babe like his own.

"He fell, ma'am, from the monkey bars. He landed on his back," he said as he tenderly handed him off to me. "I didn't see you around, but I knew he was someone's son. I think he just got the breath knocked out," the kind dad explained.

"Thank you so much. I didn't see him fall," I said while assessing my boy.

"I did," he said, patted my son on the shoulder, and walked away.

My son was gasping for breath, searching for the wind that was knocked from him. He recovered while I wiped his tears and spoke soothing words.

My mind raced with what-ifs. *What if he'd broken his arm?* and *Why wasn't I watching him? I didn't even know he'd fallen.* I berated myself.

"I knew" I heard in the back of my mind. It was a gentle reassurance, a soft reminder that God is always watching. He cares about the tiny sparrow and the flowers in the field. He cares for my children, even more than I do.

He knows the trials they will face when I'm not there. He will hold their hand when they are alone, afraid, without me to protect them.

He sees them when they fall.

He picks them up like a babe and ministers to them.

Because that's what dads do.

Matthew 6:25-27

Therefore I tell you, do not worry about your life, what you will eat or drink; or about your body, what you will wear. Is not life more important than food, and the body more important than clothes? Look at the birds of the air; they do not sow or reap or store away in barns, and yet your heavenly Father feeds them. Are you not much more valuable than they? Who of you by worrying can add a single hour to his life?

Prayer

Thank you, God, for being my father. You are always with me. You won't leave me alone. Thank you for sending your only son. I love you, Abba. Amen.

4 1

On Being a Mother

Motherhood brings me the greatest pleasure.
I love the curious questions, the soft skin, and the birth of a sense of humor. I adore their hand finding mine and watching them grow. Their companionship is a gift. I love the giggles and grins, the belly laughs that make me glow. God, thank you for the laughter of my children.

Motherhood brings me the greatest pain.

On sleepless nights, I worry over a feverish babe and the bully at school who is pestering my child. I struggle with the angst of second-guessing when I discipline and the consistency of following through. I push against the birth of rebellion and the defiant words from an angry child. These moments break my heart in two.

Motherhood is everything I thought it would be. *And more.*

I love them so much it hurts. Joy unspeakable. For years, I asked God to make me a mother. Watching my children grow out of their clothes and into their faith is one of the highlights of my life. Motherhood is God's most amazing gift to women.

Motherhood is not what I thought it would be.

I pray to God for wisdom. I cry into the night, sorry for my faults. I fear so much. I know so little. I quietly curl up beside their sleeping frames because they are too big to carry.

I'm not the mother I thought I'd be. Disappointment and regret cling to me. I seek forgiveness and wisdom when sleep doesn't claim me.

Some days I feel like I'm living my little girl dream: I'm mothering. I'm doing it well. Some days I feel like I'm living a nightmare, unhappy with the quarreling and bad choices, both theirs and mine.

But *every* day, with the easy, carefree moments or the sticky, challenging ones, I'm thankful for his mercies: new every morning. And his faithfulness endures forever.

Lamentations 3:22-23

It is of the LORD's mercies that we are not consumed, because his compassions fail not.

They are new every morning: great is thy faithfulness. (King James Version)

Prayer

Thank you, God, that in your divine plan, you created me to be a mother. There are good days, full of joy, reward. There are bad days, filled with pain and heartache. I thank you for both. Help me lean on you and seek out your wisdom. Amen.

42

Simply Living, Living Simply

My life has been shaped by moments. Monumental moments. One was a God encounter with a family from the Persecuted Church, cast out of Uzbekistan for telling others about Jesus. They came to America alone as religious refugees. They carried their babies into an unknown place, with an unknown language.

These people have become our dearest friends, our lives intertwined here on earth and for eternity. I have learned so much about simple living from this family who lives simply. When I first realized how little they had in America, I decided they needed more stuff (because aren't we good at filling our homes and our hearts with more, more, more?).

They resisted. Instead they chose the road of taking only what they need. I didn't understand their choice until I went to Africa. I met hundreds and saw thousands of impoverished people, people without stuff. Even though it wasn't their choice to have so little, I saw a pure desire to use only what they need, share the rest, and thus, find a less cluttered path to God.

We have so much, *too much*. It distracts us from him. Our abundance and opulence create a chasm away from God. We fill the void, the quiet moments, with shopping trips and the latest fashions instead of with him. The very things we fill our lives with rob us of joy and serve as obstacles on our journey toward God.

It's so easy to get caught up in The American Dream: a life that is better, richer, fuller. My Uzbek friends choose to live simply in a wealthy nation *so that* they can be generous to others.

I want a simple life. I crave simplicity. After I returned from Africa, I saw the excess in my home, the closets filled with "seasonal" décor, every wall covered, and the pattern of just replacing whatever I tired of. I opened my closet, filled with too much for one person. It turned my stomach.

I'm in the process of simplifying. I want to show my children that *more isn't better*, that *bigger isn't greater*. I want their path to God to be free from the entrapment of stuff. I want the stinginess that has consumed my life to be replaced with generosity. I want my children to be generous.

Mark 4:23-25

Are you listening to this? Really listening? Listen carefully to what I am saying—and be wary of the shrewd advice that tells you how to get ahead in the world on your own. Giving, not getting, is the way. Generosity begets generosity. Stinginess impoverishes. (*The Message*)

It turns out Africa wasn't the only one impoverished.

Prayer

I want to know you, Jesus. It's hard to find you at times because my life is so cluttered with stuff, things that only distract me from you. Help me refocus on you. Forgive me for filling my life with more of material things and less of you. Amen.

4 3

When I Am Not Nice

As it turns out, I am not always nice.

We decided to go out to eat in a *real* restaurant a few weeks ago. Now, before you conjure up images of fine dining, let me define a "real" restaurant: an eating establishment without a playground or ball pit and with free crayons. We're not brave enough to risk more.

I noticed that my husband was on his cell phone as the waiter took us to our table. I whispered, "Is that important?" and pointed to the phone. He whispered back, "Just catching up on my voicemail."

The waiter asked for our drink orders, and my hubby, still occupied, pointed to his drink order from the menu. I twitched.

"Do you want chips and salsa?" the waiter asked. I motioned for my hubby's attention, mouthing and miming chips and salsa.

He shrugged. I sent the waiter away. I was mad.

My hubby closed his cell phone and patiently listened as I spewed dinner etiquette in hushed tones. He closed his phone and put it away, offering a sincere apology. He moved on. But I wasn't quite ready.

Because sometimes I am not a very nice person.

We always split entrees at restaurants so that we don't overeat and don't spend a fortune. But, this time, I refused.

I thought our kids had been completely ignoring all of this until my daughter looked at me and said, "You're not sharing because you're mad." Her tone spoke volumes. She returned to her coloring sheet.

Well, that got to me, but I continued to be irritated throughout the meal, making snarky little comments at every opportunity.

Because I am very mature.

We finished, paid a much larger than normal bill, and walked out. But rather than feeling full and happy, I felt miserable. I couldn't stand myself another minute. I apologized to my spouse and then to each of my kids.

"Would you forgive me for acting so terrible at dinner?" I asked. Weight lifted as I tried to remember what I was even mad about.

Anger: It's ugly. It separates us from God. I often find that my lack of patience ignites my temper. It's a short fuse to an ugly me. I don't want to be impatient and irritable. I want to be like Jesus. But in my humanity, I struggle to nip this weakness at the root.

As a child, I memorized the verse in James that says we should be "slow to become angry." It often comes back to me when my anger flares, reminding me to hush and to slow down my anger.

I'm still working on the whole "nice" thing.

James 1:19-20

My dear brothers, take note of this: Everyone should be quick to listen, slow to speak and slow to become angry, for man's anger does not bring about the righteous life that God desires.

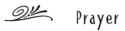 Prayer

Lord, you are so patient with me. You offer me limitless grace and patience. Help me to offer those around me the same gift. Teach me to be slow to speak and slow to become angry. I truly desire to be like you. Amen.

44

Parenting Fail

The squabbling and arguing were driving me crazy! I couldn't take another minute of fighting between my seven- and nine-year-old. There was always a bit of sibling rivalry between my older daughter and my son, but I'd reached my limit.

"That's it!" I said in a voice that even got the dog's attention. "Take it outside. I don't want to hear another word!" And then I said something that even surprised me: "Go ahead, duke it out! You guys have been pushing each other's buttons all day. You want to fight? Go at it. I'll bring the popcorn!" I shut the back door behind them and *locked it.*

My hubby looked at me like I'd just birthed an alien.

"I read about it in a parenting book. The author said the kids usually just end up laughing and working it out," I said nervously.

Hubby and I grabbed front-row seats and peeked through the curtains.

I watched my daughter, older and stronger, tower over my son. I put my hand on the doorknob. My hubby put his hand on my arm.

"Why did I do this?" I worried. "He won't stand up for himself, and she'll just keep at him!"

And that's about the time my son hauled off and punched my daughter right in the face. Seriously.

We brought them both in, my son crying and looking scared and my daughter completely in shock.

That didn't go exactly as planned, but what happened next between my kids was amazing: there was hugging and crying and loving. Reassurance and forgiveness given and ice applied. They worked it out beautifully.

But we threw that chapter on parenting out after we told our kids we'd never try that experiment again!

Bottom line: I don't know what I'm doing most days. I buy parenting books, listen to radio programs, and ask advice all the time. I make mistakes daily. But I try to learn from them, do what works, and admit when I'm just plain old wrong.

The best thing I can offer is prayer. God created my children; he knows what works and what doesn't. He gives wisdom to those who lack it (raising my hand).

James 1:4-6

Perseverance must finish its work so that you may be mature and complete, not lacking anything. If any of you lacks wisdom, he should ask God, who gives generously to all without finding fault, and it will be given to him. But when he asks, he must believe and not doubt, because he who doubts is like a wave of the sea, blown and tossed by the wind.

Prayer

Father, some days are just hard! But when I am weak, you are strong. Please grant me wisdom in parenting my children. Show me, lead me in righteousness and, please, forgive me when I mess up. Amen.

4 5

God Is in the Storm

My husband and I had driven separate cars to church that day. He had our infant son tucked in his truck, and our toddler daughter babbled in the back of my car. The sky grew darker by the second.

I wanted to get Sunday dinner started before the menacing clouds dumped their heavy raindrops. I thought I could beat the storm as I pulled in front of our townhome. I grabbed my toddler and motioned to my husband that I was going to make a run for it. He shook his head to let me know he was going to stay put.

Just as I ducked under the porch overhang, the sky opened and huge, heavy drops beat against the earth. But before I could get the heavy screen door open, the wind picked up with a frightening force and hail plummeted from the sky. To open the metal door, I would have to step out from the protection of the porch, into the raging storm with my toddler, unprotected.

I tried to wave at my husband for help, but the large tree in our yard blocked our view of each other. He was oblivious, thinking I'd made it inside. My little girl began to whimper.

Pieces of ice were striking the ground with force, so I leaned my daughter against the door and covered her with my body. Adrenaline pulsed through my veins as quarter-sized hail pummeled my back and legs.

I could feel my daughter's trembling body under mine. "Are you OK, honey? Are you hurt?" I screamed above the wind. "I'm OK, Momma," she whimpered. "I scared."

I comforted her as the raging storm soaked us both from head to toe. We shivered and clung to each other. I prayed for a reprieve in the storm.

And just as quickly as the heavens had opened, they closed. I pulled open the heavy door, fumbled for my keys, and we both collapsed inside the door. "I'm so sorry, honey, so sorry," I said as I cried. I searched her little body. "Does it hurt? Are you OK?" She pointed to a small bruise on her calf, a mark from the storm.

My husband came in and found us—a dripping, hysterical mess—and took over. I peeled my soaking clothes off and gasped at the marks that covered my back and legs. I hadn't even felt the pain.

The image of me doing everything I could to protect my child from the storm was seared into my mind that day. My instinct took over, and I was oblivious to my own risk.

Years have passed and life has brought other storms. Circumstances have raged around me, and I've been afraid. But in the midst of the storm, there was one who covered me with his protective arms, took stripes on his own back to keep me safe, to heal my brokenness.

We are mothers. It's our nature to prevent, protect, and provide for our own. But when the storm threatens *us* and *we* need to be protected, he is with us in the storm.

He is with us in the storm.

 ## Hebrews 13:5-6

"Never will I leave you;

　　never will I forsake you."

So we say with confidence,

"The Lord is my helper; I will not be afraid.

　　What can man do to me?"

Prayer

Jesus, you are with me in my darkest moments. You are with me when I'm afraid and alone. Thank you for loving me so much. Thank you for not forsaking me. Help me in the storms of this life to rest in your care. Amen.

46

Just Call Me Martha

If my phone rang *right now* and it was Jesus saying he was coming over to visit, do you know what I'd do first?

Sweep. I'm a nervous sweeper. I'd also probably throw a cake in the oven. I bet he'd like lemon. If I had time, I might even take a shower and put on a church dress.

We are talking about *Jesus* here.

I'm really good at serving the son of God. I like the way it feels to do something good for others, for him. I like my hands to be busy, my mind racing with the to-dos on my list.

But I'm not as good at seeking the son of God.

I find it easier to serve than to seek.

Martha had the same problem. Jesus was *at her house,* and she was griping because her sister wouldn't help her in the kitchen. Jesus is reading my mail in this Bible story. I get Martha, the server, fretting about her to-do list and worrying about her sister who isn't helping.

But I long to be Mary the seeker. Mary, content to leave the dirty dishes, to listen to her master. I think Mary knew in her heart that the time with Jesus was precious. She knew that nothing else mattered. Housekeeping could wait.

There's nothing wrong with serving. It's good; it's *needed*. But I think I confuse the two sometimes. I serve him, others, and I love how it makes me feel. It's rewarding.

But he is the reward.

The blessings of helping and doing are great and the earthly rewards are fantastic. The feelings that accompany "doing unto others" are wonderful. But those aren't the reward.

He is the reward.

And he's just waiting for me to put down my broom.

Matthew 6:32-34

For the pagans run after all these things, and your heavenly father knows that you need them. But seek first his kingdom and his righteousness, and all these things will be given to you as well. Therefore do not worry about tomorrow, for tomorrow will worry about itself. Each day has enough trouble of its own.

Prayer

Oh, Lord. I spend so much time doing. I like to help others. Sometimes you just want my hands to be quiet, for me to lean in and be with you. I need your help, Jesus. I confess my desire to fix things. Please teach me your ways. Amen.

4 7

Raising Children with a View of the World

Nothing shakes your world like returning from a third world country that is riddled with disease and poverty. Nothing makes you question yourself, your motives, and your own sanity more than trying to blend your old worldview with your new.

Nothing makes you want to raise compassionate children like meeting people the world has forgotten.

I have amazing kids. They are sweet and well-behaved (most days), but they are typical American children. They have too much. They want things instantly and easily. They think about themselves first.

They look a lot like their parents.

After returning from my heartbreaking and hopeful trip to Africa, I knew I had to change the way we lived. I wasn't motivated by guilt; I was moved by compassion.

My kids love to play follow the leader. They follow their parents. We've just been showing them the American view: bigger houses, nicer cars, more toys, and fitting God into all that stuff.

On a Saturday, I explained to my kids that we would be giving up the occasional house cleaner who made our life easier. I taught them to clean toilets. "Why are we doing this again?" my daughter asked. I pointed to the faces of the four children we were sponsoring through Compassion International, smiling down from their pictures on our refrigerator.

She wiped a strand of hair from her eyes, nodded, and went back to scrubbing. She stopped and said thoughtfully, "Mom, I'd like to fill the front of our refrigerator with pictures of children from all over the world."

It turns out my children were just waiting for their leaders to show them the world. They love praying for a new country at dinner every night. They can't wait to write to the kids we sponsor. They understand the choice to buy secondhand clothes and less stuff so that we can make our money matter more.

I thought the changes we made in our home would be hard for my kids. I thought there might be resistance. But they love the view and the pictures on our refrigerator.

James 1:27

Religion that God our father accepts as pure and faultless is this: to look after orphans and widows in their distress and to keep oneself from being polluted by the world.

Prayer

Lord, I love you. I want to be like you. I want my children to love others. I want them to be compassionate people. I know that we are saved by grace through faith and not by our works, but I pray that my works are evidence to the world of what you are doing in me. My children are following me; please help me lead them to you. Amen.

48

I'm Just a Girl

I hung up the phone and checked "call the roofer" off my two-page to-do list as I clicked "send" on an e-mail to my daughter's teacher. I grabbed chicken out of the freezer to defrost for dinner and then picked up the phone again to make my son an eye appointment. The doorbell rang, and I signed my name to accept packages for my husband's job.

I caught a glimpse of myself in the entryway mirror. I stopped. I smoothed my hair and rubbed at the smudges under my eyes. The weight of all my responsibilities as wife and mother was evident in my face. I looked tired.

And then I said out loud for no one but my own ears, "I'm just a girl." My mind reminded me of my mile-long list of adult duties, refuting my statement.

For a moment, I separated myself from my titles: wife, mother, daughter, sister, friend, writer, room mom, housekeeper, laundress, overall errand-runner, and keeper of the budget. It was just God and me.

I whispered (*this time* to him), "Sometimes it all feels like too much, and I don't know what I'm doing. I'm in charge of three children who need me all the time. I don't give my hubby enough attention. I worry about money and job security. I wonder about the future and fret about everything. I'm just a girl, God."

And that's when I felt his fatherly arms. They slowly wrapped me up in a quiet tenderness. I felt the easing of a heavy burden I was never meant to carry around.

Somewhere in the busyness of my life, my ministry to my family became my burden. I fretted about things I couldn't change and worried about things I didn't know. I regularly borrowed from tomorrow. It was time to give it to God. His hands were meant to hold my burdens and anxieties. They are just the right size.

Mine are too small. I'm just a girl.

1 Peter 5:6-7

Humble yourselves, therefore, under God's mighty hand, that he may lift you up in due time. Cast all your anxiety on him because he cares for you.

Prayer

Oh, God, you are so mighty. You are bigger than all my troubles. You are greater than my hectic life and many responsibilities. I cast my cares on you. Thank you for caring for me. Amen.

4 9

My Ruined Life

I never wanted to go to Africa. As a matter of fact, I grew up hoping God wouldn't send me there. As a girl, I would sit in church and listen to the occasional missionary story about faraway places, and I would feel like they were talking directly at me. It scared me.

At my Christian college, I watched my dear dorm directors give away and sell off their possessions as they prepared to go to Africa. Their table and chairs filled my first kitchen. For months, every time I sat down, I thought of their sacrifice. I finally got rid of their dinette set. I didn't like the feelings it stirred. They scared me.

A few months after I started my blog, I met a popular blogger who would become my mentor. In disbelief and awe, I read as she traveled to Africa to live-blog poverty for Compassion International. I did not envy her. Although I was compelled to sponsor our first child, I didn't want any part of Africa. It scared me.

I watched my only sister, my twin, go through the long, tedious, and emotionally exhausting process of adoption with her family. I stood back and watched, afraid of the unknown for them, scared that Africa had finally come to me. As I held their precious adopted girl in my arms, I fell in love with her and with a small piece of Africa.

Months after her homecoming, I received an unexpected phone call on a Saturday morning. It was an invitation from Compassion International to come to Africa to live-blog their relief efforts in one of the world's largest slums.

I could have said no. But *I couldn't say no.* Africa found me.

I returned from a hut in Africa to a shallow life and hobbies that filled empty hours. I returned different. I returned *ruined* for my old life. The attraction of acquiring more and more stuff sickened me. The desire to upgrade my life faded, replaced with an insatiable hunger to help the poor.

I never wanted to go to Africa. Now, I can't imagine my life without it. I'm not scared anymore.

What scares you? Sometimes the very thing that we are afraid of is what brings us the greatest freedom. In our clean, convenient, affluent world, we often shy away from the downcast, the poor, those who are different. They scare us. But when we reach out to these, we will be blessed.

Luke 14:12-14

Then Jesus said to his host, "When you give a luncheon or dinner, do not invite your friends, your brothers or relatives, or your rich neighbors; if you do, they may invite you back and so you will be repaid. But when you give a banquet, invite the poor, the crippled, the lame, the blind, and you will be blessed. Although they cannot repay you, you will be repaid at the resurrection of the righteous."

Prayer

Jesus, you didn't call me to be safe and clean in this life. You called me to follow you. I admit, I'm scared of the unknown. I'm afraid of what is different. Please help me trust you. Give me the courage to follow you wherever you lead. Amen.

5 0

Embracing My Child's Strong Will

She is the loud one at the table. She's easy to spot. Her face is smudged with chocolate because she snuck a cookie before lunch. Her hair is wild, matching hair bow long gone. Her feet are bare, socks under the table, feet tucked beneath her. She screams, "Noooo!" in a naughty voice.

The mother warns in a stern voice.

Eyes stare and heads turn to look at the noisy, unruly toddler. Her mother hushes, wipes, and bends to pick up a stray sock for the third time. She forces a smile, on the outside.

On the inside, she struggles with wanting her child to conform. To sit nicely, to behave well, to eat sandwich before cookie, to be like the other quiet children in the restaurant.

She is *me. What they think of her they think of me.* I am embarrassed by my child and ashamed that I am embarrassed.

Why do I want my child to be like everyone else? Why am I so uncomfortable with imperfection? Why is conformity more comfortable? Why do I see myself in her?

I am a double standard. I want my daughter to be comfortable in her own skin, to be herself. As she grows from a toddler to a child, I want her to know who she is. As she becomes a young lady, I want her to stand firm in truth, to withstand the strong current of worldliness that will fight to whisk her away. I want her to use her will for good when the crowd pressures her for bad.

One day, I will marvel at her strength when she makes a good decision and leads rather than follows. I will raise my head proudly when her accomplishments are made known, and I will smile when she uses her strong voice.

Yet right now, I want her to be compliant. How can I want both?

God, forgive me for wanting to squeeze her into a box. She doesn't fit. Help me embrace her strong will as a strength, not a weakness. God, may her strong will come under your control, formed into meekness, like velvet over iron.

You created her *in your image.* And she is mine.

Jeremiah 29:11

"For I know the plans I have for you," declares the LORD, "plans to prosper you and not to harm you, plans to give you hope and a future."

Prayer

God, I thank you for my child. She is your creation, and you have blessed me by making me her mother. But even blessings can be coupled with challenges. Please give me patience and wisdom in training her to be like you. Amen.

5 1

When Stuff Doesn't Satisfy

"Mom, can I go with you to the store, please?" my daughter asked. I reminded her that I was just getting groceries, nothing more. "No toys, just things we need."

"But I need lip gloss and a new bracelet."

I gave her The Look.

"OK, never mind." She ran off. I sighed.

I don't blame my kids for their affinity for stuff, for *more*. I look at the collection of miniature houses gathering dust on a shelf, the unopened craft projects I might get to, someday, clothes in various styles and sizes, stuff at every turn.

So many objects fill my home, but they do not fill my heart. I'm temporarily satisfied by the instant rush that buying brings. But when I have to toss out things I've grown tired of to make room for new things I don't need, something is wrong. Stuff doesn't satisfy.

But I'm normal, right? It's my American right to have what I can buy, and there's not even guilt if I purchase it with cash instead of credit. This is the American way: the land of convenience and the home of abundance.

But what if the American way is wrong? What if our mounds and piles of stuff only distract us from a greater purpose, from giving more to others and keeping less for ourselves?

I've found on my short, painful quest of finding a simpler life that it's much easier to start with less than to get rid of more. I think of the rich young ruler who obeyed the commandments, but when Jesus asked about his stuff, he got his feathers ruffled. "Get rid of my stuff and give it to the poor?" He walked away sad because he loved his stuff. He walked away with his wealth. But he walked away impoverished.

Do you have stuff, or does it have you?

Luke 18:22-25

When Jesus heard this, he said to him, "You still lack one thing. Sell everything you have and give to the poor, and you will have treasure in heaven. Then come, follow me."

When [the rich young ruler] heard this, he became very sad, because he was a man of great wealth. Jesus looked at him and said, "How hard it is for the rich to enter the kingdom of God! Indeed, it is easier for a camel to go through the eye of a needle than for a rich man to enter the kingdom of God."

Prayer

Jesus, I live in a world of stuff. It surrounds me on every side. It bombards me everywhere I go. Please help me remember that I am not of this world; I'm only here temporarily. I don't want my stuff, my wealth to own me. Amen.

52

The Making of a Mother

I tucked a wisp of hair behind my firstborn daughter's ear. I gazed at her freckled nose, her long lashes, and the fire in her eyes to be first and best. I prayed an unspoken prayer over her, one that asked for guidance for me and a servant's heart for her and ended with gratitude for this child that I so wanted.

And I thanked God for making me her mother.

I wrapped my arms around my son's gangly frame, breathed in his little-boy scent and returned his jab with my elbow. I laughed at his noisy giggle and dirt that stained his hands. I swallowed the lump in my throat when I thought of his sensitivity, both a flaw and a gift. I quietly prayed that God would protect his heart, bless his meek spirit, and grant him courage for this child that I needed.

And I thanked God for making me his mother.

I gathered up my boisterous toddler and held her for as long as she'd allow, tracing my finger along the outline of her round face. I rejoiced at her request for Butterfly Kisses and peppered her chubby cheek with my lashes, eyes closed. I praised God for her life and her strong will, a mixed blessing. I asked for patience for me and a yielded will for this child for whom I had prayed.

And I thanked God for making me her mother.

Three times, I have been given a child to mother and hold, and one waits for me in heaven. But when I hear the word *mother*, I don't think of myself.

I think of my own mom who is still teaching me. I hear her words in *my* voice, her warnings in *my* tone, and her love in *my* embrace.

And I thank God for giving me my mother.

1 Samuel 1:26-28

As surely as you live, my lord, I am the woman who stood here beside you praying to the LORD. I prayed for this child, and the LORD has granted me what I asked of him. So now I give him to the LORD. For his whole life he will be given over to the LORD.

Prayer

God, of all the gifts you've given me, my children are my heart. I love them fiercely, but I return them to you. You created them. You love them more than I do. I trust you with their lives. Amen.

Read more from Kristen Welch at
www.wearethatfamily.com

Author royalties from this book will benefit
The Mercy House

After traveling to Kenya, Africa, in the spring of 2010, Kristen had a strong sense that God wasn't finished with her. She and her family, along with Maureen Owino, a former sponsored Compassion child, are opening a maternity home in Kenya in late 2011. The Mercy House will exist to provide alternative options for pregnant girls living in the streets of Kenya. The Mercy House will aid the unmarried girls in nutrition, housing, prenatal care, counseling, job skills, and biblical teaching for sustainable living. The proceeds from this book will help make that goal possible. You can learn more at www.themercyhousekenya.org.